This Book
has been presented to the
CHURCH LIBRARY
of ZION LUTHERAN CHURCH

Belvidere, Ill.
In Honor Of Their
45th Wedding Anniversary

by

MR. & MRS. KEN. WARDEN

August   1985

Johann Sebastian Bach

Hannsdieter Wohlfarth

Johann Sebastian Bach

Translated by Albert L. Blackwell

Fortress Press
Philadelphia

1340

Lutterworth Press
Cambridge

Dedicated to my children Andreas, Sebastian, and Hendrika.

Published in German by Verlag Herder GmbH & Co. KG, Freiburg im Breisgau, Federal Republic of
Germany, copyright © 1984.
English translation copyright © 1985 by Fortress Press.

Library of Congress Cataloging in Publication Data

Wohlfarth, Hannsdieter.
   Johann Sebastian Bach.

    Translation of: Johann Sebastian Bach.
    1. Bach, Johann Sebastian, 1685–1750. 2. Composers—
Germany—Biography. I. Title.
ML410.BlW763 1985   780'.92'4 [B]   84-47916

Fortress edition: ISBN 0-8006-0736-8   Lutterworth edition: ISBN 0-7188-2617-5
2900 Queen Lane   7 All Saints' Passage
Philadelphia, Pennsylvania / USA   Cambridge CB2 3LS / England

K963H84   Printed in the Federal Republic of Germany   1-736
Pictures: Ost und Europa Photo, Cologne
Offset reproduction: H. & H. Schaufler, Freiburg im Breisgau
Printing: Freiburger Graphische Betriebe 1984

CONTENTS

Childhood and Youth 7
New Duties 15

Illustrations, Section I: Origins and Youth 17–28
Illustrations, Section II: The Arnstadt Period 37–44
Illustrations, Section III: Capellmeister in Weimar and Cöthen 53–64

The Court Capellmeister 66
The St. Thomas Cantor 80

Illustrations, Section IV: Leipzig and Dresden 81–88
Illustrations, Section V: Late Works, Journey to Berlin, Sons 97–104

Chronological Table 114
Index of Illustrations 117

Childhood and Youth

Peace reigned in Germany. Yet everywhere memories remained alive of the terrible war that for thirty years had wasted the land and caused horrific losses among the populace. Grandparents told grandchildren of it, warning them thereby against regarding peace as something to be taken for granted. Children were instructed in the fear of God and in moral living so as to avoid rekindling God's wrath and thus imperiling the peace. In the perception of that age God stood at the center of the world as Ruler; this "theocentric" world view determined every happening on earth.

This world view also determined the position of music, understood as a wondrous creation of God that should therefore resound primarily *laudatio Dei,* to the praise of God, as St. Augustine had earlier advocated. The divine, mathematically regulated world order found its resonating image in music, and the pious performer or the reverent listener was richly graced with a *recreatio cordis,* a healing of heart and spirit. The Thuringian music theorist Andreas Werckmeister (born in the same year as Bach's father, Ambrosius) expressed this outlook in a work of 1686:

That *musica* or *harmonia* has its origin from God and has been granted to humanity as a glorious gift from the Creator is not something known and understood by many spiritual and learned theologians alone, for the thoughtful heathen were also able to recognize it by their common sense. Thus the aims of music are glorification of God, inducement of virtue, and legitimate refreshment for the spirit.

A powerful voice, steeped in faith, speaks to us through these words. And nowhere in late seventeenth-century Europe was this world view, with its Augustinian perception of music, still so unbroken and vital as in Thuringia, home of the reformer and one-time Augustinian monk, Martin Luther.

This perception also ruled the thoughts and activities of the extensive Bach family of musicians, whose members had for many generations occupied the most important positions of organist and cantor in Thuringia, and frequently positions of court musician and town piper *(Stadtpfeifer)* as well. Whether in Erfurt or Arnstadt, in Ohrdruf, Schweinfurt, or Eisenach, "the Bachs" were bearers of a musical tradition, and at annual family days they proudly strengthened their togetherness. In this connection Johann Nikolaus Forkel, author of the first Bach biography, reports:

As it was impossible for them all to live in one place, they resolved at least to see each other once a year and fixed a certain day upon which they had all to appear at an appointed place ... Their amusements, during the time of their meeting, were entirely musical. As the company wholly consisted of cantors, organists, and town musicians, who had all to do with the Church, and as it was besides a general custom at the time to begin everything with religion, the first thing they did, when they were assembled, was to sing a chorale. From this pious commencement they proceeded to drolleries which often made a very great contrast with it. For now they sang popular songs, the contents of which were partly comic and partly naughty, all together and extempore, but in such a manner that the several parts thus extemporized made a kind of harmony together, the words, however, in every part being different. They called this kind of extemporary harmony a *Quodlibet*, and not only laughed heartily at it themselves, but excited an equally hearty and irresistible laughter in everybody that heard them.

The town piper Johann Ambrosius Bach, formerly of Erfurt, lived in Eisenach from 1671. As a respectably trained artisan he belonged to a guild, enjoyed civic rights, administered house and property holdings, and distinguished himself accordingly from the itinerant musicians, jugglers, and beer-hall fiddlers. Together with his four colleagues, he was required as part of his regular duties "to pipe at the town hall twice a day, middays at ten o'clock and evenings at five o'clock." Also he was required "on all feast days and Sundays, before and after the sermon at morning and afternoon worship, to wait upon the instructions of the cantor." This cantorship belonged to a kinsman and great musician, Johann Christoph Bach, praised in the family chronicle as the

View of Eisenach. Copper engraving by M. Merian, 1650.

Johann Christoph Bach the elder,
uncle of Johann Sebastian.
Anonymous painting.

"great and expressive composer," who at the time occupied the office of cantor at Eisenach's St. George Church.

Johann Ambrosius Bach was a capable town piper or *Hausmann*, as he was also called because of his duties at the town hall or *Rathaus*. The Eisenach town chronicle reports of him: "At Easter of 1672 the new *Hausmann* performed with organ, violin, voice, trumpets, and military drums as no other Eisenach cantor or *Hausmann* has ever done." He was familiar with almost all instruments, and there was no major town festival in those years to which he and his colleagues did not add musical luster.

The ability of Ambrosius immediately came to the attention of Prince Johann

Georg I of Saxe-Eisenach, then residing in Eisenach, and from 1677 the town piper Bach also served in the prince's capelle as court musician. That Ambrosius led an upright life is confirmed by a town council report required by the prince after Ambrosius had sought the right to brew a certain quantity of beer tax-free. We read in the report: "The new *Hausmann* has not only devoted himself to a quiet Christian mode of life pleasing to everyone, but has also distinguished himself in his profession to such a degree that in vocal as well as instrumental music, at worship and at honorable gatherings, with persons of high and low estate, he can render good enjoyment, so that, so far as our memory extends, we can recall nothing comparable in these parts."

The marriage of Ambrosius Bach and his wife Elisabeth née Lämmerhirt produced seven children, two of whom were daughters. The oldest son, Johann Christoph, was already fourteen years old and had just begun instruction with the famous organist Johann Pachelbel in Erfurt, when on 21 March 1685 the youngest child was born and two days later baptized as Johann Sebastian. The baptismal font is still to be seen today in Eisenach's St. George Church. Martin Luther had once preached in the same church as he returned in 1521 from the Diet of Worms. In the year 1221 Elisabeth von Ungarn, later canonized, was married to the Thuringian Count Ludwig IV in the same place. The baptized's uncle, Johann Christoph, played the organ at the christening service. Up to that time he was considered the most profound composer of the great Bach family. Today, after three centuries, he would probably be forgotten—were it not for that baptized infant!

We may assume that the small Johann Sebastian was offered musical instruction as soon as he possessed the requisite maturity. That father Ambrosius taught him violin is an established fact. Sebastian attended the Latin school from his eighth year on and served as a chorister in worship—at first in the itinerant boys' choir *(Kurrende)*, in which unison hymns were sung, later in the *chorus symphoniacus,* in which he gained intimate knowledge of polyphonic motets, sacred concertos, and cantatas. As a result of numerous choir rehearsals and various other musical obligations Sebastian could attend school only irregularly—in the year 1695 he missed no fewer than 103 school hours! Nevertheless, he was soon at the top of his class and in Latin outstripped his brother Johann Jakob, three years his senior.

When Sebastian was nine years old his mother died; shortly before his tenth birthday he lost his father as well. His oldest brother, twenty-four-year-old Johann Christoph, who had become organist in Ohrdruf, took him and Johann Jakob into his family. Johann Christoph also undertook the musical instruction of his youngest brother, giving him a foundation in clavier and organ playing and presumably in the basic rules of composition as well. In the latter, the arts of chorale setting and of aria-variation and toccata and fugue composition, which Johann Christoph had learned earlier with Johann Pachelbel, must certainly have served as standards. As a chorister Sebastian contributed to the family's support. At times the child's passion for learning must have been absolutely unsettling. We are told, for example, that Johann Christoph denied his brother's earnest desire to study Christoph's collection of clavier pieces by contemporary composers, since according to pedagogical plan they were still too difficult. The young Sebastian, however, is said to have secretly copied out the pieces at night by moonlight, only to be surprised at the task by his brotherly foster father and punished by confiscation of the almost-completed manuscript.

Sebastian remained in his brother's house in Ohrdruf for five years. In the Latin school, where he was instructed primarily in Latin and Lutheran orthodoxy, he was repeatedly best in his class, and at the early age of fourteen he reached the top level; most of his classmates were three years older. But at this time Johann Christoph fell upon such economic straits, as a result of an abundance of blessings in the form of children, that the brothers taken in as foster children had to look for other places to live. Johann Jakob returned to Eisenach to enter into an apprenticeship as town piper with his father's successor. For Johann Sebastian, however, fate held another path.

At the turning of the year 1699/1700 the pealing bells greeted both a new century and a year that would prove to be one of the most significant for the further course of young Sebastian's life. Elias Herda had returned home to Thuringia at that time to take up duties as school cantor in Ohrdruf. He informed his eighteen-year-old friend Georg Erdmann and Erdmann's school comrade, Johann Sebastian Bach, about the northern German town of Lüneburg with its cloister school of St. Michael, at which he had been trained as a scholarship student. He could also report on an excellent choir at St. Michael's, the matins choir *(Mettenchor)*, constantly in need of good voices, especially treble ones. A youth who was skilled in singing, could perhaps also play an instrument, and was in addition, in the words of the statutes, "a child of the poor" who "otherwise had no means of support," stood a good chance of being accepted at St. Michael's. The students were assured free room and board, even a bit of pocket money, but above all outstanding training in the scholarly disciplines. This all sounded so enticing that Sebastian and Georg Erdmann, who was three years older, importuned the cantor to apply for them in Lüneburg. The conditions of admission could certainly be met: both of them were poor and vocally gifted. The recommendation by Elias Herda achieved the desired result. In mid-March 1700, just before Sebastian's fifteenth birthday, the two friends set out on foot for Lüneburg, 350 kilometers distant. We read in the Ohrdruf school records concerning Sebastian, "Luneburgum ob defectum hospitiorum se contulit die 15 Martii 1700," that is, "as a result of lack of support he betook himself to

Lüneburg on 15 March 1700." In April, Bach's name appeared in the school register of St. Michael's.

After the coming of the Reformation to Lüneburg in 1531, the former Benedictine cloister of St. Michael had at first been converted into a Protestant seminary. Since 1656, however, its buildings had housed a boarding school for young noblemen. From that time it was called the Knight's Academy *(Ritterakademie)*. It nevertheless included ten to twelve scholarship positions for nonnoble but vocally talented youths, who, along with several older scholarship students, constituted the matins choir. This choir, supported by instruments, was responsible for the festive embellishment of worship services. Motets, cantatas, and oratorios resounded with regularity. The music library of St. Michael's, begun in 1555 and steadily expanded since, was rich in works of the preceding century and a half. Among them were also compositions of the Bach family!

Thus the young Sebastian, who was soon entrusted with the position of choir prefect, became acquainted with the entire spectrum of church-music styles developed since the latter part of the sixteenth century. Besides the old but still vital style of polyphony, monody—an expressive accompanied melodic line—and the concertizing style, with all its varieties and special forms, were preeminent. Also, fine organ music was to be heard in Lüneburg, particularly at the Church of St. John, where Georg Böhm served as organist. In Lüneburg Sebastian certainly found further opportunity to develop and perfect his performance on violin, clavier, and organ—abilities first acquired in Ohrdruf. Instruction in the school of St. Michael included the subjects of Latin, Greek, and Lutheran religion as well as logic and rhetoric. The last of these was principally the offering of Rector Johann Büsche, who lectured twice a week "de inventione e rhetoricis doctrina." Decades later, in 1738, the Leipzig professor of rhetoric Johann Abraham Birnbaum was to declare of Bach, "his insight into the arts of poetry and rhetoric is as good as one could possibly ask of a great composer." We may assume that the determinative basis of Bach's understanding of music as an *ars rhetorica* was established during his Lüneburg school years.

At that time the interest in French culture played a predominant role in the Knight's Academy. This was manifested first of all in language training. The young noblemen were obliged to speak French with one another, as French was then the language of the court and diplomacy. Another aspect of French culture involved the practical command of the complicated court dances which, in spite of their manifold formal configurations, were always to be performed with unfailing elegance and grace. A certain Thomas de la Selle was employed as dancing-master at the Knight's Academy. As a former student of the great Jean-Baptiste Lully, court capellmeister to King Louis XIV, he was an eminent authority on the art of French dance and the suite. The names of the dance forms are still familiar today: allemande, courante, sarabande, menuet, gavotte, bour-rée, gigue, and many others. This Thomas de la Selle was at that time also engaged as a violinist by Duke Georg Wilhelm von Braunschweig-Lüneburg in neighboring Celle, whose court was a virtual outpost of French culture. The Duke's music-loving wife, Eleonore Desmier d'Olbreuze, had brought with her from her French homeland a group of excellent musicians, who for the most part performed French music of the late seventeenth century, under the direction of their capellmeister Philippe La Vigne. They played compositions by Lully, Marchand, de Grigny, d'Anglebert, d'Andrieu, Dieu-part, Le Bègue, and the great François Couperin, among others.

Thomas de la Selle and the young Bach soon became friends. Several times they traveled together to Celle, where Sebastian eagerly took advantage of the many rich opportunities offered. The effect of these impressions from Celle was lasting, leading Bach to become in time one of the greatest and most versatile masters of the suite. He also became acquainted with French organ music in Celle, preparing for his own use a copy of the *Livre d'orgue* by Charles Dieupart. Thus, although Bach never visited France, he was able to study the French style in Celle as if at the source, appropriating it as an additional and valuable ingredient of his own artistic resources.

View of Lüneburg. Copper engraving by M. Merian, 1654.

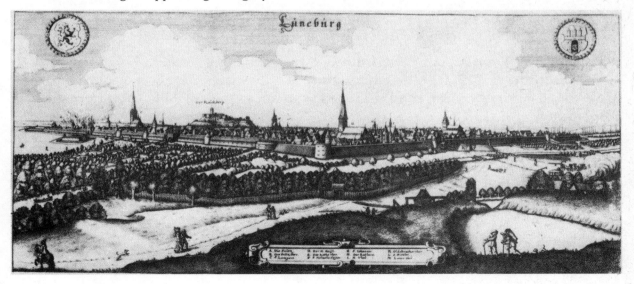

13

The years of Lüneburg schooling held in store yet another enrichment as well. In Hamburg lived the elderly Jan Adams Reinken, a famous organ improvisator, a former teacher of Georg Böhm, and one of the last representatives of the Netherlands school of organ playing, founded in Amsterdam by Jan Pieterszoon Sweelinck. The sixteen-year-old Bach visited Reinken in 1710 and listened enraptured to his improvisation on the chorale "By the Waters of Babylon." Sebastian also sought out the Hamburg opera.

Thus a superabundance of stimulation was available to Johann Sebastian Bach during his Lüneburg student years, and the soil upon which this stimulation fell was uniquely fertile. Bach's later mastery was grounded in a complete command of craftsmanship, still regarded in his day as learnable by students with talent and industry. *Exempla*, selected from the masters, were imitated by the student, enabling him to become a master in turn. Bach's theocentric world view, in which the *ordo ecclesiasticus* and the *ordo saecularis*—church and world—still comprised a unity, offered no place for the "original genius" characterized in the late eighteenth-century's understanding of art. In his willing study and emulation of the masters' works we see the young Bach as a musician standing firmly upon the foundation of venerable, unbroken, living tradition. His principles of learning and creating were still congruent with the axioms handed down to him by his forefathers. An instruction book in composition from 1643, the treatise *Musica poetica* by the Nürnberg music theorist Johann Andreas Herbst, states:

If one wishes to produce and perfect something fruitful and useful, then it is necessary that he industriously examine the *cantiones* and songs of the most distinguished and renowned musicians or composers, marking well the laws of part-writing and notation they have followed, learning to imitate and emulate them with power and facility, until he is so well exercised and trained in the masters … that he can bring forth similar works from his own mind and abilities.

These were the principles Bach followed in becoming a master.

At Eastertide of 1702 the Lüneburg student years came to an end, and Sebastian again found himself on the road to his Thuringian homeland. But he returned home transformed.

New Duties

Having ended his student years the seventeen-year-old Bach had to look for a settled position. Yet the year 1702 offered no beginning of great significance for his career. From earliest childhood he had always been obliged to provide at least part of his up-keep from his own labors, at first as a singer in the itinerant boys' choir and a member of the church choir, later as choir prefect in Lüneburg. Moreover, we may assume that during his extensive travels he probably performed as a fiddler in guest houses and vil-lage squares to pick up a few coins. As a member of the Bach clan, and particularly as the son of a town piper, he was accustomed to performing readily wherever he was needed.

At the same time we must realize that 1702 marked the close of his student years only in the most formal sense. To be sure, Johann Sebastian Bach had by that time already acquired a broader musical knowledge than any other member of his extensive family. But we know that his learning never came to an end. Throughout his life, wherever he went he appropriated and creatively transformed every artistic stimulation that offered itself. This remains true for his mature work as well, which in retrospect appears to us as the magnificent climax of centuries of Western polyphonic development, but which also influenced the future by shaping musical creativity in a multiplicity of essential ways, from the late eighteenth century right up to the present moment.

One might object here that the "old" Bach proved obstinate and unreceptive to the *buffo* style of a Pergolesi, streaming from the south so enticingly since about 1730—that Bach ceased to learn. Let it be answered that Bach's creativity made it possible for a Mozart to transcend the Neapolitan *buffo* style, with its fleeting cheerfulness, and as-cend to the noble language of classicism. Not only do Bach's stylistic roots extend deeper into the past than those of his contemporaries, they influence the future more richly as well. Without Bach twentieth-century music would likely have taken on a quite different appearance, so deeply has it been influenced by Bach's musical heritage.

In historical perspective, then, the year 1702 proved to be less a caesura in Bach's life than a point at which the young composer resolved to move on to new duties, responsi-ble to and confident in himself. The way was clear. His lifework could now commence.

As Bach was returning to Thuringia, three organist positions had become vacant and were in need of being filled: at the Church of St. Jacobi in Sangerhausen; the Church of St. George in Eisenach, where Bach had been baptized; and the Boniface Church in Arnstadt, residence city of the count. It is not known whether Bach applied to succeed his famous uncle Johann Christoph Bach in Eisenach; in any case, not he but his cousin Johann Bernhard Bach was appointed to that position. He did apply in Sangerhausen, however, and upon completion of a successful audition even won approval of the town council. But no invitation was forthcoming. Duke Johann Georg of Saxe-Weissenfels decreed that the established court musician Johann August Kobelius rather than Bach should be appointed to the organist post. Thus Bach turned to Arnstadt.

The Boniface Church of Arnstadt had been rebuilt after a conflagration of 1581, and was commonly called the New Church thereafter (today, the "Bach Church"). For a long time, however, funds for a new organ had been lacking and a positive organ had sufficed as a temporary instrument. But at the beginning of 1703 a great new organ from the workshop of the Mühlhausen organ builder Johann Friedrich Wender stood almost completed, and employment of a suitable organist was required. Until the completion of the organ, without which not even the requisite audition was possible, the young Bach had to look for suitable interim employment. This he found in Weimar with Duke Johann Ernst, a younger brother and coregent of Duke Wilhelm Ernst of Saxe-Weimar. He joined Johann Ernst's small private orchestra under the official title of "Lackey," presumably as a violinist. He also replaced the court organist Johann Effler, by then quite elderly and ailing, and we may assume that he became acquainted with the violinist Johann Paul von Westhoff, employed in Weimar and numbered among the most celebrated European violinists of the age. This grand artist and virtuoso, also prominent as a Saxony diplomat and language teacher at the University of Wittenberg, first developed double-stop playing and created the first polyphonic work in several movements for unaccompanied violin, his "Suite pour le violon seul sans basse" of 1683. Perhaps Bach received here the stimulus for his later sonatas and partitas for solo violin.

The illustrations of the following pages:
 1) Road to Wechmar. Here lived Veit Bach (d. 1619), progenitor of the family.
 2) Johann Ambrosius Bach, father of Johann Sebastian.
 3) The Bach House in Eisenach.
4/5) Rooms in the Bach House, Eisenach.
 6) View in the St. George Church in Eisenach.
 7) The Ehrenstein palace in Ohrdruf.
 8) Interior view of St. Michael's Church in Lüneburg.
 9) The palace of Celle.
10) View of Hamburg.
11) Jan Adams Reinken, Hamburg organ master.

Bach's Arnstadt audition on the now-completed Boniface Church organ went so brilliantly that the church consistory decided to forgo the auditioning of other candidates. Bach subsequently negotiated so confidently and adroitly that he easily succeeded in obtaining the authorities' promise of a yearly wage of fifty guilders, with an additional thirty talers for expenses and dwelling. This was exceptionally propitious financial support for a beginning position, particularly when we realize that Bach, at the age of eighteen and still single, was beginning with a higher income than most of his forebears had attained in their lifetimes.

Bach assumed his church duties on 9 August 1703. The Certificate of Appointment reports in part: "You are ... in your daily life to cultivate the fear of God, sobriety, and the love of peace; altogether to avoid bad company and any distraction from your calling and in general to conduct yourself in all things toward God, High Authority, and your superiors, as befits an honor-loving servant and organist." Next to God, the highest Arnstadt authority was Count Anton Günther of Schwarzburg and Hohnstein, Lord of Arnstadt, et cetera, et cetera. Bach, however, had nothing to do with this sovereign directly. Instead his dealings were with the town elders, particularly the church consistory, at that time under the leadership of Superintendent Gottfried Olearius.

The chief duty of the organist was to accompany the congregation in chorale singing. In addition to the main Sunday worship service, a Monday prayer service and an early service of preaching on Thursdays from seven to nine o'clock were stipulated in Bach's contract. The contractual duties were thus not very extensive. There was no cantor to whom the organist was responsible.

Bach took quarters in the lodging At the Golden Crown. Some of his relatives lived there as well, including a distant cousin, Maria Barbara Bach, of about Bach's age, to whom the young organist soon took a cordial liking. Life in the little residence city, decorated with well-tended public gardens might have been idyllic, had not difficulties arisen within a short time between Bach and the church consistory. These were kindled by confusion concerning provisions for a choir. Although Bach's contract made no stipulations concerning a choir, the church authorities wished to have a choir for the main worship service. So, as the Boniface Church had no permanent choir, Bach had to assemble a small choir from the students of the town's Latin school and rehearse them for the Sunday performances. These students, who were completely undisciplined and had little inclination for music besides, provoked Bach's anger to such an extreme that matters finally came to blows. A student named Geyersbach, who was almost as old as Bach himself and whom Bach had already nicknamed "Nanny-goat bassoonist" (Zippelfagottist) attacked the choirmaster one day, striking him with a cudgel, whereupon Bach drew a sword. The brawl was quickly brought to an end thanks to the vigorous intervention of Bach's near-relative, cousin Barbara Catharina Bach, who was later called to testify as a witness. But Bach's relationship with this school choir had been permanently disrupted and with it his collaboration with the church authorities.

Among the rebukes Bach received in Arnstadt was the accusation that he had once allowed a "strange maiden" to perform music in the church. As this could not possibly refer to a service of worship, perhaps Bach had taken one of his cousins into the church to perform a cantata aria or a sacred song as he practiced the organ. Certainly she might have sung with more feeling and musical taste than that of the Latin school singers! But in that time women were still not allowed to sing in church—not even as members of a choir. In support of this prohibition the church appealed to the word of Paul, "mulier taceat in ecclesia"—"women should remain silent in church." Cloisters of nuns were the only exceptions to this rule.

The final break with the consistory was precipitated in 1706 by an occurrence that belongs in an artistic sense among the young Bach's most beautiful and determinative experiences. News of the great organist and composer Dietrich Buxtehude, cantor at St. Mary's in Lübeck, may already have reached Bach's ear in Lüneburg, giving rise to his abiding wish to visit this master. In the fall of 1705 Bach asked the consistory for a special leave of absence for this purpose, to be limited to four weeks' duration. The consistory granted his request. The Arnstadt church authorities must have foreseen the honor that would accrue from having a student of the famous Buxtehude as their organist. Bach's cousin Johann Ernst Bach was engaged as his substitute.

We can perhaps imagine Bach's glad expectation as he set out for Lübeck and the enthusiasm that must have seized him as he saw Lübeck's much-admired silhouette emerge from the late autumn haze. For several promising weeks his Arnstadt responsibilities, often so oppressive, lay behind him. Before him, his long-desired encounter with the great Buxtehude and his artistry!

Until this time Bach had known and studied primarily the organ compositions of Pachelbel, Böhm, and Jan Adams Reinken. The treatment of the chorale in Buxtehude's work, however, differed in several respects from that of these masters. Pachelbel typically treated phrases of the hymn melody fugally. Böhm and Reinken inclined more to a free "coloration" of the melody, decorating it with an abundance of rhythmic notes playing around the principal line. Buxtehude, however, had developed a new type of setting in the "chorale fantasy." Here the chorale melody was reduced to its individual phrases, provided with contrapuntal companion motifs, and these elements were then worked into an artistic whole. Buxtehude treated the traditional chorale melody as a kind of quarry providing him building materials from which his masterful hand then

Chorale arrangement
(BWV 739) from the Arnstadt
period, perhaps Bach's
earliest extant musical
manuscript.

created a work that was both liturgically appropriate and stood on its aesthetic merits as well.

Besides Buxtehude's organ artistry, Bach must also have been enticed by the famous evening concerts *(Abendmusiken)* that were a specialty of Lübeck's musical life of that time. Buxtehude's predecessor, Franz Tunder, had initiated these evening concerts upon beginning his tenure as cantor of St. Mary's Church in 1641. They had at first served simply as entertainment for merchants awaiting the market's opening. But in 1668 Buxtehude had shifted them to Sundays—specifically, to the last two Sundays of Trinity and the second, third, and fourth Sundays of Advent. At the same time he had enhanced them artistically, conceiving of them as performances for an appreciative audience in their own right, apart from any service of worship. Music was here performed and listened to for its own sake, in a wholly modern sense. It is true that according to one official document the evening concerts were "to thank the Most High God at year's end by the finest of means, including musical, for all the good He has bestowed." Still, it is clear that more numerous and more gifted musicians were generally available for the evening concerts than for services of worship. Some forty excellently trained singers and instrumentalists participated.

Bach's visit in Lübeck was so happy that without great scruples he extended his stay from four weeks to four months. Perhaps he hoped to be able to step in as successor to Buxtehude, now almost seventy years old. The old master would certainly have concurred. An unwritten but nonetheless binding law of St. Mary's Church at that time, however, required that the post of cantor could go only to a person who in addition to possessing great professional ability was also willing to marry his predecessor's daughter. J. Mattheson and G. F. Handel, who visited Lübeck in 1703, had already foundered on this stipulation. Mattheson had written: "Because a marriage stipulation was proposed, for which none of us had the least desire, we departed thence, after having received many attestations of honor and many culinary entertainments." Nor was Bach prepared to marry Buxtehude's daughter, ten years his senior and not particularly charming, and thus Buxtehude was forced to stay at his post into advanced age.

Bach returned to Arnstadt where an antagonistic hearing before the high consistory awaited him. The inexcusable overstaying of his leave by a quarter year was obviously a weighty cause for complaint. Even more a matter of reproach was Bach's completely altered style of accompanying congregational singing. The congregation was shocked enough by Bach's playing of free fantasias between the verses of hymns, but that he accompanied the hymns themselves in the style of a chorale fantasy brought even sharper protest. We read in the minutes:

Reprove him for having hitherto made many curious *variationes* in the chorale, and mingled many strange tones in it, and for the fact that the Congregation has been confused by it.

And he was admonished:

In the future, if he wished to introduce a *tonus peregrinus,* he was to hold it out, and not to turn too quickly to something else, or, as had hitherto been his habit, even play a *tonus contrarius.*

Bach submitted to these demands, obeying them "to the letter" by limiting himself to the barest necessities; this led to new reproofs. He had already secretly resolved to free himself of his Arnstadt duties as soon as opportune circumstances arose. When Johann

Georg Ahle, organist of Mühlhausen's St. Blasius Church, died in December 1706, Bach and some of his relatives contacted the authorities there to arrange audition invitations.

On 24 April 1707, an Easter Sunday, Bach appeared before the consistory and the council of the free imperial city of Mühlhausen and once again inspired the enthusiasm of his listeners with magnificent organ playing. Negotiations were soon entered, issuing in a marked salary increase. The official appointment followed on 15 June. As an imposing expert on organ building, Bach also expressed his wishes for improvements of the St. Blasius organ, which the council at once granted. "No one has ever tried out organs so severely and yet at the same time honestly as he. He understood the whole art of organ building in the highest degree." So Carl Philipp Emanuel Bach later testified to the great expertise of his father.

The Mühlhausen post guaranteed Bach a firm financial basis, and when in addition a small legacy followed upon the death of his uncle Tobias Lämmerhirt, his mother's brother, nothing stood in the way of marriage with his beloved Maria Barbara from Arnstadt. On 17 October 1707, Johann Sebastian and Maria Barbara Bach entered the bond of matrimony in the little village church of Dornheim near Arnstadt. Two famous sons were to issue from this marriage: Wilhelm Friedemann, born in 1710, and Carl

Capriccio (BWV 992) on the departure of brother Johann Jacob Bach (1706).

Philipp Emanuel, born in 1714. The latter especially has taken his place in history as an important pioneer of the Viennese classical style.

Immediately upon his official arrival in Mühlhausen, Bach immersed himself in a rich musical life. His involvement even extended to the church music of neighboring towns. Above all, his first significant compositions now were composed, especially in the realm of the cantata. Only a few compositions had been written in Arnstadt. All of those still extant are works for keyboard instruments (organ, harpsichord, clavichord).

Of special interest among these Arnstadt works is the "Capriccio sopra la lontananza del suo fratello diletissimo" ("Capriccio on the Departure of His Most Beloved Brother"). Bach's brother Johann Jakob, who with Sebastian had been taken in by their oldest brother in Ohrdruf following the death of their parents, had decided in 1704 to join the Swedish army as an oboist. Such a wish must have seemed particularly daring at that time, as Sweden was conducting a war against Russia and also against Russia's ally Saxony, the homeland of the Bach family. Accordingly, Jakob's friends and relatives had attempted to alter his decision, but in vain. All of this—the pleading, the lamenting, and finally the departure with its postilion horn call—is represented in this musical composition with the most affecting eloquence. The composition inspired Goethe's enthusiasm, leading him to remark:

It is a marvelously simple melody, appealing to the imagination—a fanfare, yet so widely, indeed, endlessly varied that we not only hear the trumpeter, now near at hand, now far away, but even seem to see him riding in the field, pausing on a rise, turning to the four corners of the world, and wheeling again on his way. Indeed we can never exhaust its meanings for our senses and spirits.

Johann Jakob Bach turned to all corners of the world in actuality. He took part not only in all the military campaigns of the Swedish king Charles XII but also in his flight to the Turks. In Constantinople he made the acquaintance of the flutist Pierre-Gabriel Buffardin, then in the service of the French ambassador to the Turkish sultan, and enjoyed the privilege of his instruction. (This same Buffardin was later the teacher of Johann Joachim Quantz, who in turn taught Frederick the Great.) Upon the restoration of peace Jakob returned to Stockholm, where he died in 1722.

In Mühlhausen Bach wrote his first cantatas, among them the brilliant "God Is My King" (BWV 71), first performed on 4 February 1708 at the celebration of the government's changeover; the cantata "Out of the Depths I Cry to Thee, O Lord" (BWV 131); and also the inspired elegiac cantata "God's Time Is the Best of Times" (BWV 106), presumably composed for the burial service of Bach's uncle Tobias Lämmerhirt. This work, known also by the name of "Actus tragicus," is on the one hand a clear example of the older middle German cantatas with their overlapping movements, oriented toward the motet, and their restriction to biblical and chorale texts (with corresponding avoidance of newly composed texts). But on the other hand this cantata is "a work of genius such as even the great masters seldom attain, and with which this twenty-two year old at one stroke left all his contemporaries far behind. ... The 'Actus tragicus' is a piece of world literature" (A. Dürr). In the middle section of this symmetrical cantata Bach has utilized the various compositional styles of his time in the full service of textual expression. He sets the Old Testament message ("It is the ancient bond: Man, thou must die!") in the old style, that is, in the polyphonic motet style. In contrast, he sets the New Testament message of salvation ("O come, Lord Jesus, come!") in the new homophonic declamatory style. On a third level, both musical *and* spiritual, the flutes simultaneously intone the chorale "I Have My Cause to God Entrusted." Thus Old Testament, New Testament, and the living congregation of Christ as symbolized by the chorale all find musical expression. This musical synthesis of polyphonic motet, homophonic sacred concerto, and chorale elaboration within one and the same movement testifies to such spiritual and artistic originality that this one work alone might have sufficed to ensure its creator's prominent place in musical history.

Organ works of significant quality also were composed in Mühlhausen. Bach endeavored to bring the church music entrusted to him to a higher level than had previously been the case. This wish was frustrated, however, by intrachurch conditions that had just entered a particularly critical stage. Opposition between representatives of orthodox Lutheranism on the one hand and of Pietism on the other had existed throughout Protestant Germany since the late seventeenth century. It manifested itself in Mühlhausen with particular intensity. The orthodox Lutheran pastor of St. Mary's Church, Bach's friend Johann Christian Eilmar, and Bach's immediate superior in the St. Blasius Church, Superintendent Johann Adolph Frohne, who inclined to Pietism, had recently split over this theological problem.

As is well known, Martin Luther's teaching was grounded in the claim of preeminence of the biblical Word over church teaching or dogma. With the rise of Rationalism and the Enlightenment in the baroque period this principle faced a serious crisis. The old concepts of faith, which were essentially irrational, had to be defended and secured against the knowledge claims of human understanding and the criteria of a modern world view grounded in sense perception. Instead of alluding to the fundamental difference of character between the truths of faith and the knowledge of reason, people were inclined to schematize the articles of faith in the manner of a system of natural science or logic, so that they might appear unassailable. In contrast, Pietism represented a simple piety, drawing its power from personal experience of God, trusting the soul's sensibility more than the critical capacities of human understanding, and authenticating itself in daily living.

Whether Bach was concerned with this intrachurch controversy we do not know. As a musician, however, he certainly inclined more to Lutheran orthodoxy, which, since Luther's time, had given highly stylized church music a privileged place in worship. Indeed, Lutheran orthodoxy perceived music as an *explicatio textus,* a means of interpreting God's Word, and as a *praedicatio sonora,* a "resounding sermon." The Pietists, in contrast, permitted music only in its simplest form as a "realm of reverence, love, and efficacious power," as J. G. Herder was later to express it. Certainly, then, when Bach inclined more to orthodox Pastor Eilmar than to Superintendent Frohne, not only personal friendship but also Bach's musicianship was a deciding factor. For Bach shared the musical experience of Martin Luther, still undisturbed by rationalistic temptations:

Music is a beautiful and lovely gift of God, a queen over every stirring of the human heart. Nothing on earth is more powerful than noble music in making the sad joyful, the arrogant discreet, the despondent valiant; in charming the haughty to humility; and in mitigating envy and hatred.

Thus the words of Martin Luther, and so too the thinking and perception of Johann Sebastian Bach.

Given the circumstances in Mühlhausen, however, Bach saw that he was not in a position to realize his conceptions of "church music well-regulated to the Glory of God." Perhaps he also wished to improve his economic status. In any case, he departed from the free imperial city before a year had passed. When on 25 June 1708 he sent his resignation request to the town council, he could proudly declare to the city fathers that he

The illustrations of the following pages:
12) View of Sangerhausen, where in 1702 Bach applied without success for an organist post.
13) View of the Weimar palace.
14) J. S. Bach. Painting by J. E. Rentsch the elder.
15) The Bach Church in Arnstadt.
16) Organ façade in the Bach Church.
17) Original Arnstadt organ console used by Bach.
18) The Dornheim Church where Bach was married on 17 October 1707.

had "received the gracious admission of His Serene Highness of Saxe-Weimar into his Court Capelle and Chamber Music." The council granted his request with regrets, asking Bach to continue his overseeing of the organ building in Mühlhausen, an offer which he willingly accepted. His cousin Johann Friedrich Bach, a son of the deceased Eisenach cantor Johann Christoph Bach, was called as his successor at St. Blasius Church. So Johann Sebastian, now a famous organist, returned to Weimar, where five years before he had served as a fiddling lackey.

Since Bach himself sometimes thought in economic categories, perhaps a purely financial note is permissible at this point. In Arnstadt Bach received an annual salary amounting to approximately 85 gulden, which, measured by the incomes of other organists in comparable positions, was already a rather lucrative amount. In Weimar his salary was to increase within a short time to at least 252 gulden, indicating that his reputation as a musician was steadily mounting. Without a perceptible aura of artistic distinction, such an improvement in his income and reputation could scarcely be accounted for.

Apart from the few months early in 1703 which Bach spent in Weimar awaiting completion of the Arnstadt organ, he was now for the first time a musician exclusively in the service of a court. This change from a church or town appointment to employment by a secular sovereign must have been a liberating experience at the time, for the spirit of the Enlightenment was more powerfully at work in a royal court than in the comparatively dull domains of town and church government. It is true that a servant to a prince had to adapt to the absolutistic mechanisms of court ceremony. But most creative artists would have been more than satisfied with belonging to an established order, being answerable to an individual rather than to a council, and finally, working in a context that offered the artist not only material security but also an atmosphere of noble refinement found only in a prince's court. This must have been especially true for a musician in the service of a music-loving prince. Where this was the case, a composer found himself in a much happier situation than most composers of today, for he did not have to be anxious that his works might never be performed.

What is more, in that prerevolutionary time nothing humiliating or servile was yet associated with service to a prince. The concept of the prince's sovereignty still rested upon the principle of God's grace and was not conceivable otherwise. The prince's lordship appeared as an image of God's lordship. The prince was legitimated as one called to earthly lordship in accordance with the divine governance of the world. Thus, as God was at the center of the world's activities, so the prince was the source of power for that kingdom granted him by divine grace. In this view, a court musician's service was understood as a spiritual vocation as well.

45

The musician, outwardly distinguished by his lackey's uniform, was bound to an invariable order of service extending to the regulation of every detail. As the planets circle the sun, so the servants of the court meshed in the mechanism of absolutistic ceremonialism. Even the composer had to submit to this regimen—although as the leader of the capelle, who could enhance the lord's renown by creating new works for him, the composer doubtless enjoyed special status among the musicians. Yet even this was not an essential distinction but merely one of degree.

All this was naturally reflected in the concept of musical art: it was understood as a *symbolon ordinis,* a symbol of order, whether cosmic order or the order of the state. Its reason for existence in the court, therefore, was to reflect aesthetically the essential splendor of divine majesty—including, of course, the princely majesty as well! Similarly with the architecture of the baroque palace, the symmetry of the palace gardens and the eternal order of the starry universe. God's creation was still understood as a well-ordered community of all God's works. Bach's great contemporary and compatriot, the philosopher Gottfried Wilhelm Leibniz, expressed it in the following words:

Like the parts of a machine, every being has its assigned place and there fulfills its particular role. Every being is related to all others; each is a living member of the universal organism. Although they differ in capacity for cognition, each—be it a stone, a plant, an animal, a beggar, or a prince— is a living mirror image of the universe, and because the universe as a whole is completely ordered by God, so complete order must also rule in each individual being. This universal monarchy is thus the most perfect government, under the most perfect of all monarchs.

"Sheep in pastures green abiding / safely with their shepherd rest; / where the sovereign ruleth wisely, / joy and peace the land have blessed." Thus the words of an aria from the "Hunt Cantata" Bach was to compose in Weimar in 1713. To be secure in a beneficent order: this still-unbroken, traditional consciousness was able to transcend the hardships of life in general and of service in an absolutistic princely court in particular, which often appear to us so onerous in that era.

Among the virtues that enhance esteem for a monarch among his people, natural dignity ranks highest. It is as far removed from mere geniality as from tyranny. The person who possesses it radiates that true authority for which no other characteristic, whether riches, strength, intelligence, or even familiarity, is an adequate substitute. Bach's new sovereign, Duke Wilhelm Ernst of Saxe-Weimar, possessed such natural dignity. He was very religious, thoroughly pervaded by the idea of God's grace in the most fundamental sense. Accordingly, he understood his governing role as nothing other than a responsibility before God. Austere in his personal mode of life, he was a friend of the fine arts and the sciences. Through his enlarging of the court library and collections, his designing of manicured public gardens, and his general beneficence, he prepared the unmistakable Weimar atmosphere that was later to inspire Goethe and bind him to this spot.

Bach was appointed court organist in the palace church and took part also in the court orchestra as *cammer-musicus* (presumably as a violinist or harpsichordist). In addition to several singers, some twelve instrumentalists belonged to the court ensemble. The ensemble had to be supplemented, according to the practice of that time, by several oboists drawn from the ranks of the military and who were thus not listed in the court orchestra roster. This orchestra was under the leadership of a director, or *Kapellmeister,* by the name of Johann Samuel Drese and his son Johann Wilhelm, who functioned as vice-capellmeister. In 1714 Bach advanced to a position of orchestra leadership under the title of "Concertmeister with official rank below that of the vice-capellmeister." We even know something about the dress of the court musicians from a chronicle of the time: "Sixteen well-trained musicians dressed in Hungarian-style livery occasionally entertained the Duke's ear."

Bach thus had both ecclesiastical and secular duties in Weimar. But in both roles he was responsible to the prince alone, and not to a church or town governing body. With his appointment as concertmeister on 2 March 1714, he was required to write a sacred cantata each month and perform it in the worship service of the palace church. The texts for most of these cantatas were by Salomon Franck, who was serving as consistorial secretary in Weimar and also administering the court library. At this same time, however, Bach also became acquainted with the cantata texts of Pastor Erdmann Neumeister, which likewise stimulated him to provide musical settings. Indeed the change from the texts of Salomon Franck to those of Erdmann Neumeister had far-reaching consequences for the formal organization of these compositions. Specifically, Neumeister, who was court deacon in Weissenfels from 1704 to 1706 and presumably attended performances of the court opera, wished to see the forms of recitative and the tripartite *da capo aria*—forms employed chiefly in Neapolitan opera up to this time— utilized also in the sacred cantata. He wrote his texts accordingly. In his own words, "I regard a cantata as nothing other than part of an opera, made up of the *stylo recitativo* and arias." He justified this substitution of operatic and madrigal texts for biblical and chorale texts with the observation that they were dedicated to the glory of God and thus could not be profane.

In their formal organization, Bach's earlier cantatas are still very close to the sacred concerto of the seventeenth century. Now he turned to the form of the Italian chamber cantata, musically related to the Neapolitan *opera seria,* as represented preeminently in the works of Alessandro Scarlatti, the prevailing operatic style of the late baroque.

Here again Bach was able to incorporate new influences successfully into his characteristic "Bach" style. His style had previously developed mainly from the German and French traditions; now in Weimar it was enriched by the Italian influence.

Nor was this influence limited to the cantata. Johann Gottfried Walther, a distant relative of Bach, was active in Weimar as organist at the Church of St. Peter and St. Paul. As a great connoisseur of Italian music he was fond of making organ transcriptions of compositions by Corelli, Legrenzi, Albinoni, Vivaldi, Torelli, and other Italian masters, adapting them appropriately in the process. He stimulated Bach to similar efforts, through which Bach became intimately acquainted with Italian concerti and chamber music. Bach thoroughly studied older Italian organ music as well, producing in the process a copy of Frescobaldi's *Fiori Musicali* (Venice, 1635). Occasional visits to performances of Italian opera in Dresden later completed Bach's knowledge of Italian baroque music.

As had already been the case with the cantata, Bach was able to blend all these novel influences of Italian art with his own artistic practices in most ingenious ways. This creative appropriation of Italian models relates not only to formal organization and the proclivity for incessant musical impulse, but also to a feeling for a supple cantabile and for the shaping of long melodic phrases. Bach understood how to join these features with his inherent gifts for counterpoint and expressive harmonization in such a way that here too works of unmistakable "Bach" greatness resulted.

Besides their preoccupation with Italian music, Bach and Walther had still another common interest that was to play a central role in Bach's later music. Both took great pleasure in difficult experiments with counterpoint. They occasionally exchanged canons of exceedingly complicated construction. One of these, the "Canon â 4 voc: perpetuus" which Bach sent to Walther on 2 August 1713, bears the inscription: "To contribute this little item at this place to the Honored Owner [of this book] in the hope of friendly remembrance is the wish of JOH. SEBAST. BACH Court Organist and Chamber Musician to His Saxon Highness." It foreshadows that later cyclical canon—one of the most abstract and at the same time most expressive pieces of the 1747 *Musical Offering* composed by Bach in homage to Frederick the Great, which spirals in constant modulation, and which Bach annotated, "ascendente modulatione ascendat Gloria Regis" ("as here the modulation ascends, so ascends the glory of the King").

From Weimar Bach formed a friendship with Georg Philipp Telemann, who served as court capellmeister in neighboring Eisenach for several years following 1709. Telemann was the sponsor at the baptism of Bach's son Carl Philipp Emanuel. After Telemann's death in 1767, C. P. E. Bach became his successor as the music director of Hamburg.

Canon (BWV 1073)
with dedication of
2 August 1713.

Although in Weimar Bach was not only organist but also active as court musician and concertmeister, most of his works there were nevertheless for church use. Besides the composition of cantatas, to which he was obliged by contract after 1714, he wrote on his own initiative an abundance of magnificent organ works during this period. These represent every genre of organ music except the organ concerto accompanied by orchestra: chorale settings and chorale partitas (variations); preludes; toccatas and fugues, among them the famous Passacaglia in C minor; and a series of other pieces, such as the Pastorale in F major, the Canzona in D minor, and the "Alla breve."

Among the chorale arrangements, the compositions collected in the "Little Organ Book" (Orgelbüchlein) assume an outstanding position. With Bach's growing fame as an organist and clavier performer the number of his students also mounted steadily. Thus he wrote the forty-five organ chorales of the Orgelbüchlein not only for his own use but also to furnish a teaching collection for his students. Other teaching collections of comparable rank were to follow later, among them the Well-Tempered Clavier and the two- and three-part Inventions and Sinfonias. The title page presents the pedagogical aim of this first collection:

49

Little Organ Book
In which a Beginner at the Organ is given Instruction in Developing a Chorale
in many divers ways, and at the same time
in Acquiring Facility in the Study of the Pedal
since in the Chorales contained therein the Pedal is treated as Wholly Obbligato

in Praise of the Almighty's Will
And for my Neighbor's Greater Skill

Autore
Joanne Sebast. Bach

The Weimar organ works written in the *stylus fantasticus*, that is, in a free style not bound to a chorale melody, are often characterized by an exceedingly tumultuous, forward-sweeping impulse bordering on improvisation or rhapsody, even in the fugues. The energy of these works, especially the toccatas—now pent-up, now breaking forth with eruptive force—must have struck Bach's contemporaries as shocking, even demonic. Toward the end of 1714 Bach made an official trip to Cassel in the company of his Duke and there gave an organ concert. Its effect was reported by a certain Constantin Bellermann, rector in Minden: "His feet flew over the pedals as if they had wings; the mighty sound roared through the church like thunder." As a rule, enthusiastic responses of this kind are not familiar to us until the romantic period. That a witness from the early eighteenth century speaks in this way gives us an indication of the effect Bach's exuberantly charged organ playing, including much free improvisation, must have exercised over his listeners. The same applies to the harpsichord toccatas of this period and to the fantasies, preludes, and fugues. One thinks here especially of the Prelude and Fugue in A minor (BWV 894) which, with the addition of a slow middle movement, Bach later reworked as a concerto for flute, violin, harpsichord, and strings. Even more, one thinks of the famous Chromatic Fantasy and Fugue in D minor (BWV 903), probably conceived in Weimar but not completed until around 1720 in Cöthen. The rationally disciplined emotion, sensual appeal, and inner grandeur we encounter in this splendid work are unrivaled in that genre and in that century.

The experience of Bach's organ and clavier music later moved Goethe to one of his most profound declarations concerning music. At first older music interested Goethe only as a historical phenomenon to which he applied himself "with pleasure, interest, and reflection." But the experience of Bach's music gave rise to an inclination based on more than mere historical interest. He believed that the same organic, evolutionary process of growth was at work both in this music and in nature—specifically, the Aristotelian principle of *entelechy,* or the continual power of growth as the indwelling goal of all life.

Indeed, Goethe's experience with Bach went even further. In 1814 Goethe was a guest in Bad Berka near Weimar, where the local organist performed Bach compositions for him. In 1827 Goethe wrote of this experience to a friend, the musician Carl Friedrich Zelter:

Well I remember the good organist at Berka; for there, in complete tranquillity of mind and without external distraction, I first began to comprehend your great master. I said to myself: it is as if eternal harmony were communing with itself as might have happened in God's bosom just before the creation of the world. So it stirred within me as well, and it was as if I no longer possessed or needed ears, still less eyes or the other senses.

Upon reading Goethe's words we see a great door opening before our eyes, as it were, offering a view into the primordial myth of the world's origin. The ancient concept of the world as a harmoniously resounding cosmos, with earthly music as its audible image, comes alive in these words. The doctrine of Pythagoras in antiquity held that the ordering principles of music are the same as those upon which the universe is based, and St. Ambrose of Milan called music an "imitation of the musical rapport among the heavenly bodies." Goethe senses this same vision upon hearing Bach's music. It is as if the epochs of Pythagoras, Ambrose, Bach, and Goethe had merged—and our own epoch as well, insofar as we are able to open ourselves to their visions, thoughts, and creativity.

Bach had lived and worked almost eight years at the Weimar court when in 1716, despite his increasing recognition as an artist of the highest rank, a noticeable worsening of relations with his duke set in. It is not possible today to ascertain unequivocally whether some particular incident occasioned this development. In any case, a series of differences soon led to the final break. Perhaps the precipitating cause is to be found within the royal family. We know that an exceedingly strained relationship existed at this time between Duke Wilhelm Ernst and his oldest nephew Duke Ernst August, who was obstinately determined to gain a share in the affairs of government. This enmity led among other things to the duke's levying a fine of ten talers upon any of his court musicians who might perform in the palace of his headstrong nephew. Duke Ernst August, who like his younger brother Johann Ernst enjoyed the privilege of lessons with Johann Sebastian Bach, admired his famous teacher so greatly that he openly favored him, often inviting him to musical collaborations in his palace. For his part, Bach also honored the duke, dedicating compositions to him and once even presenting him with a poem of homage.

All this could not have remained unknown to the reigning duke, and soon Bach experienced his royal wrath. Specifically, Bach was not named as successor upon the death of the old capellmeister, Johann Samuel Drese, on 1 December 1716. Instead, Telemann was first offered the post, and upon his refusal the offer went to Drese's son Johann Wilhelm, who gladly accepted. Bach was so disappointed that from then on he composed no more cantatas for the Weimar court, and also refrained from participating in the Weimar festivities that were to take place in 1717 on the occasion of the two-hundredth anniversary of the Reformation.

Meanwhile Bach had been on the lookout for other possible positions. His friendly relationship with Duke Ernst August, though the cause of his Weimar misery, now proved useful to him. At the beginning of 1716, Duke Ernst August had married a sister of Prince Leopold of Anhalt-Cöthen, and through her Prince Leopold must certainly have come to know something of Bach's outstanding abilities as a composer and performing artist. The leader of the Cöthen court orchestra was to retire on 1 August. So it happened that Bach was asked to take over the position. Bach accepted eagerly, and his appointment as "Capellmeister of His Royal Highness the Prince of Anhalt-Cöthen" followed promptly on 5 August 1717. The prospects must have seemed bright to Bach. Prince Leopold, who at twenty-three was nine years younger than Bach, was known to be exceptionally fond of music. Accordingly, he employed an admirably accomplished musical staff, several of whom had previously served in the royal court capelle in Berlin.

The illustrations of the following pages:
19) St. Mary's Church in Lübeck.
20) View of Mühlhausen.
21) Organ of St. Blasius Church in Mühlhausen.
22) Palace chapel in Weimar.
23) Duke Johann Ernst of Saxe-Weimar.

JOH. SEB.
BACH
★ 1685 † 1750
FÜRSTL. CAPELLMSTR.
ZU
CÖTHEN
1717—1723

Concerto 5to. à une Traversiere

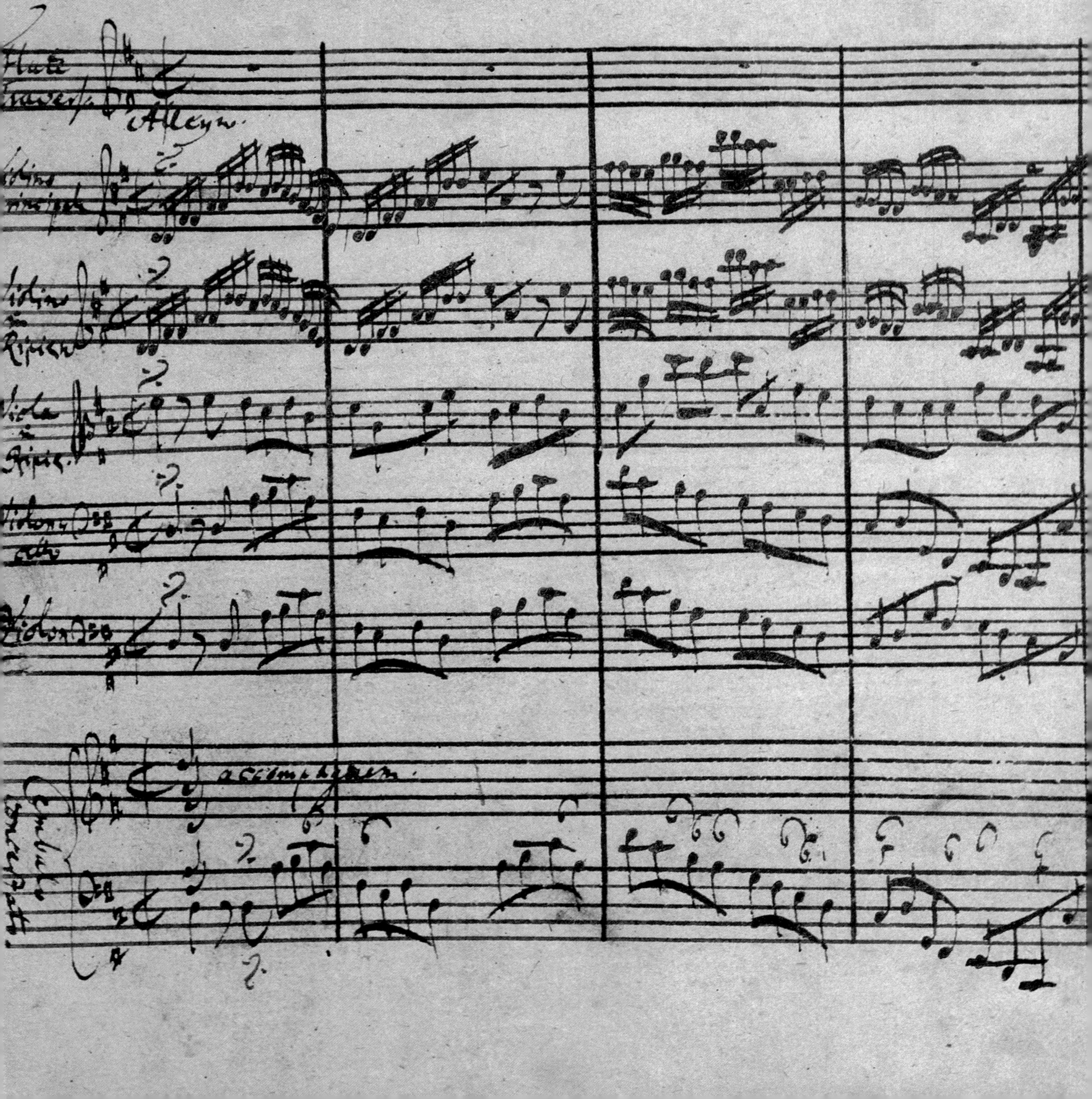

ne Violino principale, une Violino è una Viola in ripieno
Violoncello, Violone è Cembalo concertato.

Bach could not assume the Cöthen capellmeister position immediately, however, as he had neglected to submit a formal resignation request to the duke of Weimar. This fact and, even more important, the fact that Prince Leopold was a brother-in-law of the detested Duke Ernst August and thus belonged to the opposition party led to Duke Wilhelm Ernst's strict denial of Bach's request. Bach learned of the ducal decision upon his return from a triumphant artistic visit to Dresden and submitted a protest. This only led to a hardening of the duke's position. When negotiations over the standoff failed to reach any accord, Duke Wilhelm Ernst had his unbending concertmeister abruptly arrested. We read in that year's Weimar court records:

On November 6, [1717,] the quondam concertmeister and organist Bach was confined to the County Judge's place of detention for too stubbornly forcing the issue of his dismissal and finally on December 2 was freed from arrest with notice of his unfavorable discharge.

Immediately upon his release Bach and his family moved to Cöthen. Prince Leopold bore the costs. Around 10 December 1717, Johann Sebastian Bach, with his wife Maria Barbara and their children, arrived at the place of his future work. A new period of his life and creativity now ensued.

The illustrations of the preceding pages:
24) Johann Sebastian Bach. Painting by J. J. Ihle.
25) Prince Leopold of Anhalt-Cöthen.
26) Bach memorial at the Cöthen palace.
27) The Cöthen palace hall of mirrors.
28) Manuscript of the Brandenburg Concerto No. 5.
29) View of the Weissenfels palace.

The Court Capellmeister

"Capellmeister to His Serene Highness the Prince of Anhalt-Cöthen" and "Director of His Chamber Music": these were now Bach's official titles. In Cöthen, at the age of thirty-two, he had reached the position generally regarded as the highest and most desirable in the musical hierarchy during that period of courtly absolutism. Bach had arrived. He was court capellmeister to a young and musical prince who loved him and marveled at his art. Bach responded to his happy circumstances with gratitude and good spirits: "There I had a gracious prince, who both loved and knew music, and in his service I intended to spend the rest of my life," he later wrote of his years in Cöthen. Cöthen fulfilled all the conditions he required for fruitful productivity: creative stimulation and recognition on the part of a sovereign who was cultured in every respect; a receptive audience; excellent instrumentalists, and opportunity for continual artistic experimentation with them. Neither earlier nor later as cantor of Leipzig's St. Thomas Church could Bach count himself so fortunate. The first three years of his Cöthen period, at least, seem a glorious interlude.

Service to the young Prince Leopold was doubtless the chief component of this artistic and intellectual climate that was so satisfying to Bach. Church music scarcely played a role in the residence city, whose population, like that of the court, belonged predominantly to the Reformed Calvinist confession. What church music there was consisted of simple congregational singing accompanied by organ. But within a short time Leopold was able to develop his court into a small, luminous center of culture. He had early lost his father, and for several years his mother, Gisela Agnes, had administered an extremely austere regency. The court ensemble had consisted of only three musicians! But since arriving at the requisite age for taking over the affairs of governance, Leopold had devoted himself to the fine arts and to the cultivation of learning. He collected art treasures and enlarged the court library. But above all he founded a splendid court capelle, for he felt himself most vitally involved in music, both as an admirer and as a connoisseur. He himself played viola da gamba and harpsichord and sang in a beautiful, trained baritone voice.

Immediately upon his accession in 1712, he traveled to Italy to seek out and personally recruit suitable instrumentalists for his court. The composer and music theorist Johann David Heinichen accompanied him as an expert advisor. After his return in the following year the prince was able to secure other highly qualified musicians as the result of an unforeseen opportunity. Namely, on 25 February 1713 the Prussian King Friedrich I died in Berlin. Thereupon his robust son and successor Friedrich Wilhelm I immediately dissolved the excellent court capelle, as its artistic demands seemed to him a waste of money and time. The instrumentalists he dismissed gladly accepted an invitation to Cöthen and, with the Italians, soon constituted one of the finest court orchestras of the time.

This capelle, in which Prince Leopold himself enjoyed playing, eventually consisted of some eighteen to twenty musicians—regarded in those times as quite an imposing ensemble. Nine of these musicians bore the title of a *cammer-musicus*, or chamber musician, whereby they were distinguished from the ordinary *musici*, who served as tutti string players. The conductor was also reckoned among the ensemble, since he did not yet direct the orchestra with a baton—as has been the custom since the nineteenth century—but rather from the harpsichord or occasionally as a violinist. It is known that Bach was fond of playing in the orchestra as a violist. Musicians from the military ranks could also be employed when required, and several vocal soloists were included as well. Normally a choir was not needed, or at most was required only to end a cantata in honor of the prince with a festive choral verse. In such cases the resources of the St. Agnus Church, founded by Leopold's mother, were available.

The founding of this church for the few Lutherans who lived in Cöthen had aroused the anger of the Reformed Calvinist consistory at the time, who even appealed to the kaiser in Vienna, asking him to revoke the establishment of a Lutheran church in a Reformed principality—albeit without success. Leopold, too, protected the religious minority within his territory. At the time of his accession to the throne, in the face of religious strife between Reformed believers and adherents to Lutheran doctrine, he had declared that it was "the greatest of blessings when freedom of conscience is protected for the subjects of the land." This protection of Lutherans in the midst of predominantly Calvinist surroundings benefited Johann Sebastian Bach and his family as he commenced his Cöthen activities in 1717.

As leader of the court capelle Bach was now a higher court official, at the marshal rank, who could live in the royal palace and eat at the officers' table rather than at the servants' table as formerly. Furthermore, his annual salary stood at about four hundred imperial talers. Bach enjoyed his new position and its accompanying esteem. He valued courtly titles and remained eager to acquire new ones. During his Cöthen period he also called himself "Royal Capellmeister of Saxe-Weissenfels," though no such specific appointment had ever taken place. As late as 1733, when he was the Leipzig cantor, he successfully applied to the elector of Saxony for permission to use the title of "Composer to the Court Capelle."

The same Bach who could strike so gruff a tone in dealings with church consistories or city councils could master the punctilious ceremonial language of a genteel courtier in the dedication to a composition written in honor of a prince. This is the case, for

Christian Ludwig,
margrave of Brandenburg
(1677-1734).
He commissioned the
Brandenburg Concertos,
which are dedicated to him.
Engraving by M. Bernigeroth.

example, with the Brandenburg Concertos, dedicated in 1721 to Margrave Christian
Ludwig of Brandenburg; or one thinks of the dedication of the *Musical Offering* (1747)
to Frederick the Great. Indeed we perceive something of this proclivity for the distinctive language of court and nobility in one of Bach's last written documents. Already
blind, Bach dictated a cover letter on 27 December 1749 to send with his son Johann
Christoph Friedrich who was pledged to the court of Count Wilhelm of Bückeburg. It
reads:

Most Highborn Imperial Count,
Gracious Count and Lord!

May Your High Imperial Grace the Count most graciously permit the presumption of my pen to lay
this present note before your exalted eyes, chiefly because I deem myself profoundly beholden to

render most humble thanks for the valued remembrance sent me by Your High Imperial Grace the Count. Also to convey to Your High Imperial Grace the Count the utmost wish that you might deem one of my children worthy of Your High Grace and receive him into your service. Thus am I sending my son with this letter, hoping that he may be in a position to do full justice to Your High Imperial Grace the Count.

Most Highborn Imperial Count,
Your High Imperial Grace's
most humble and obedient servant
Johann Sebastian Bach

As a member of the inner circle of courtly pomp Bach accompanied his prince on his annual trips to Bohemian Carlsbad, particularly popular with the European aristocracy of that time. He may have first met the margrave of Brandenburg on one of these trips. How completely Bach had become a part of the courtly world becomes clear from the list of godparents who appeared at the baptism of his seventh child, Leopold Augustus, in 1718. The Cöthen church register reports: "The godparents were (1) His Most Serene Highness Prince Leopold, reigning Prince of Anhalt; (2) His Most Serene Highness Prince Augustus Ludwig, Prince of Anhalt; (3) Her Most Serene Duchess Eleonora Wilhelmina, Duchess of Saxe-Weimar by marriage, Princess of Anhalt by birth." Besides these three members of royalty, two members of the lesser nobility served as additional sponsors. (Not all of this nobility, however, could prevent the baptized from dying only ten months later.)

In Cöthen, in accordance with the needs of the court, Bach composed and performed chamber music almost exclusively. Only for New Year's Day and the prince's birthday did he have to write occasional sacred and secular cantatas. Oratorios and operas were apparently not performed in Cöthen.

"Chamber music," "musique de chambre," or "musica da camera"—whatever its designation, it was music artistically performed in the royal chambers before an elite circle of listeners. At that time chamber music was not yet a generic classification; rather it was a cultural and sociological phenomenon. For instance, in the seventeenth and eighteenth centuries chamber music designated a particular musical event arranged for a strictly circumscribed class of listeners and presented in a room especially provided for and accessible to them alone. In this purely external way chamber music in the period of courtly absolutism distinguished itself from the comparatively public musical performances of theater or church. Even today the term chamber music connotes an exclusive sphere.

In Bach's time the term "chamber style," like the term *musica reservata* in the sixteenth and early seventeenth centuries, designated a particularly artistic compositional genre fully appreciated only by the connoisseur. It demands "far more diligence," said

Johann Mattheson in 1739, than do other kinds of music. The same exclusivity that caused the prince's court and nobleman's palace in this era of courtly absolutism to appear as a self-enclosed world apart—an artistic paradise from which all unpleasantness was banned—determined the essence of chamber music as well. At the same time, however, courtly chamber music represented one of a very few points of contact between musical professionals and princely dilettantes. The musical prince was united with his musicians into a chamber music ensemble in order to submit in common to the artistic will of the court composer and capellmeister. Where else would such a "symbiosis of classes" have been thinkable in the age of courtly absolutism?

Most of Bach's extant chamber works were written in Cöthen: the flute and violin sonatas with figured bass accompaniment, and also the sonatas with obbligato harpsichord; the viola da gamba sonatas; and the trio sonatas for two melody instruments (violin, flute) and figured bass. The six sonatas and partitas for solo violin "senza basso accompagnato" are rarities of special value. Bach composed these pieces in 1720, possibly for the Dresden court violinist Johann Georg Pisendel. In them we see Bach's creative inclination to exploit the most extreme technical possibilities of an instrument—in this case polyphonic playing on the violin—to produce works of the richest artistic content. The six suites for solo violoncello are similar. Bach probably wrote them for the Cöthen court musician Christian Ferdinand Abel. In both collections we experience a degree of inner polyphony and artistic breadth that surpasses many other composers' works written for several separate voices. They remained unrivaled throughout their age.

Chamber music of that time also included orchestral music composed for the court. Here belong Bach's four great Orchestral Suites, patterned upon the French style; the violin concertos; the Triple Concerto in A minor; and the magnificent "Six Concerts avec plusieurs Instruments" sent by Bach in March 1721 to Margrave Christian Ludwig of Brandenburg and consequently known as the Brandenburg Concertos. These works reveal anew Bach's desire to enjoy to the full all the compositional possibilities offered by a given form, in this case, the Italian concerto grosso. Each of these superb concertos represents a wholly independent and novel solution of the concerto phenomenon. This applies both to their instrumental scoring and to their formal structure, and above all to the individual character of these six works.

We cannot know today how many Cöthen compositions have been lost. Since the account books from Bach's period of service indicate scarcely any purchase of music written by other composers, we may assume that much more of Bach's music was played than we now possess.

In addition to his duties at court Bach was continually occupied with teaching his students, among whom his own sons were particularly talented. To his friend Georg Erdmann, Bach wrote proudly of his sons: "They are all born musicians and make it possible for me to arrange an ensemble both *vocaliter* and *instrumentaliter* within my own family." On 22 January 1720 Bach began compiling a "Little Clavier Book" *(Klavierbüchlein)* for his son Wilhelm Friedemann, almost ten years old. It exemplifies a masterful graded-lesson series for clavier. Simple instructions in fingering and ornamentation are followed by small pieces, some by Bach and some by other composers. Finally come the "Preambles" and "Fantasies" that later, after revision, became known as the two- and three-part *Inventions and Sinfonias.*

Naturally the "Little Clavier Book" was used in teaching other students as well. Thus, as Bach did not consider teaching gifted students an unpleasant task but rather allowed teaching to inspire his creativity, so too work at the instrument was by no means limited to the transmission of technical dexterity. The creative impulse was always at work. The students understood that these clavier pieces which they had to master technically were also models for their own future compositions. Bach exercised the patience and watchful understanding of a true teacher. He did not injure his students. Rather, like a good gardener, he cultivated the soil without damaging the roots.

Bach's teaching methods are well known to us from reports left by his older sons, Wilhelm Friedemann and Carl Philipp Emanuel, and by several of his students, principally Johann Philipp Kirnberger and Johann Nikolaus Gerber. Bach always began his instruction with technical studies at a keyboard instrument, preferably at the most sensitive of them, the clavichord, which served as preparation for the organ as well. The first months of instruction were concerned with exercises in touch, fingering, and the various kinds of ornamentation. Then these abstract technical exercises were replaced by little pieces, carefully suited to the student's stage of manual development, which, it is reported, were sometimes written out during the lesson hour. These little exercise pieces led to more complicated works, combining use of previous clavier styles with attention to polyphonic interplay of voices—or, in Bach's own words, the art of managing "obbligato parts correctly and well." This formulation is found in the foreword Bach added to the second copy of the two- and three-part *Inventions and Sinfonias.* It reads:

Upright Instruction
wherein the lovers of the clavier, and especially those desirous of learning, are shown a clear way not alone to learn to play clearly in two voices, but also, after further progress, to deal correctly and well with three *obbligato* parts; furthermore, at the same time not alone to have good *inventiones* [ideas], but to develop the same well, and above all to arrive at a singing style in playing and at the same time to acquire a strong foretaste of composition.

Here again we see how closely related creativity, composition, and instrumental performance were for Bach. He strikes us as the *musicus perfectus*, in whom theoretical knowledge, creative power, and practical ability were still inseparable. In addition, Bach felt called to transmit such a great gift through teaching!

Bach considered the proper basis for composition to be instruction in figured bass, which he regarded as "the most perfect fundament of music." He understood a musical work from this foundation upward. The bass, not the upper voices, determined the harmonic modulation of phrases; the bass secured compositional unity. Here we find one of the most important differences between Bach's musical conception and the musical understanding of the post-baroque period. In post-baroque musical language the monodic events of the upper voice, rather than the bass, become central. This alteration in musical understanding was to play an essential role in the lives of the Bach sons.

In the summer of 1720, in cheerful spirits, Bach once again traveled to Carlsbad with Prince Leopold and several members of the court capelle. They enjoyed the charming landscape and the magical atmosphere of the mineral baths, far from the duties of the capital. The return trip in early July was full of confidence. But upon his arrival at home Bach was met by sad and distraught children. Their mother, Maria Barbara, was dead. Carl Philipp Emanuel was to recall later:

After thirteen years of blissful married life with his first wife, the misfortune overtook him, in the year 1720, upon his return to Cöthen from a journey with his Prince to Carlsbad, of finding her dead and buried, although he had left her hale and hearty on his departure. The news that she had been ill and died reached him only when he entered his own house.

We do not know much about Maria Barbara. Neither the sons nor other contemporaries have furnished us with testimony, and in the face of so private a moment modesty restrains us from speculating in print concerning the emotions of Johann Sebastian upon his sad homecoming. It is sufficient to give rein to our fantasy, silent and unwritten.

His experience of July 1720 suddenly returned Bach to the world of church music that we might have thought forgotten. When the post of organist at the St. Jacobi Church in Hamburg became vacant in the same year, Bach immediately applied for the position. For the audition on 28 November, to which he and eight other musicians were invited, he composed the Fantasy and Fugue in G minor (BWV 542). Among the three Hamburg organists who were to make the choice was Jan Adams Reinken—the same master whom Bach had once visited from Lüneburg—now ninety-seven years old. At the time of that earlier visit the sixteen-year-old Bach had heard Reinken's improvisation on the chorale "By the Waters of Babylon." Now Johann Sebastian rendered this

The Jacobi Church
in Hamburg.
Engraving, c. 1700.

same chorale in his audition on Reinken's organ in Hamburg's St. Catherine Church. This time the elder, almost a hundred years old, listened enthralled to the master from Cöthen. When Bach had ended his playing Reinken said to him: "I thought this art had perished, but I see that in you it still lives!"

It appears that the Hamburg church council endeavored to hire Bach as the St. Jacobi organist. That Bach did not accept the position may plausibly be attributed to two possible reasons. First, Bach had originally hoped to receive the position of "City Music Director" along with the duties as organist. A second cause of his refusal may relate to a peculiar practice of the Hamburg church authorities at that time—namely, the typical trading zeal of that Hanseatic city extended even to the conferring of the organist positions, in that the candidate was preferred who declared himself ready to show his gratitude by the largest contribution to the church's coffers. In other words, the post of organist could be bought!

There were, it is true, men of the Hamburg church who took exception to this abuse and sought at least a compromise. Thus we read the following entry in the minutes of 21 November 1720:

There were many reasons not to introduce the sale of an organist's post, because it was part of the ministry of God; accordingly the choice should be free, and the capacity of the candidates should be more considered than the money. But if, after the selection had been made, the chosen candidate of his own free will wished to give a token of his gratitude, the latter could be accepted for the benefit of the Church and the Holy Sepulcher, entered in the books, and used again where it was needed.

A "free-will" contribution was thus expected and materially affected the outcome of the selection. When Bach, who was repelled by this practice, manifested no further interest in the Hamburg organist post, the consistory called "the son of a well-to-do artisan, who was better at preluding with his talers than with his fingers," as Johann Mattheson later remarked.

The pastor of St. Jacobi's at the time, Erdmann Neumeister, many of whose cantata texts Bach had set to music, was particularly indignant over this course of events. He found occasion in his next Christmas sermon to voice his views concerning the practice of purchasing positions. In connection with the angel choir's singing at Christ's birth, he said he was firmly convinced "that even if one of the angels of Bethlehem should come down from heaven, one who played divinely and wished to become organist of St. Jacobi, but had no money, he might just as well fly away again."

So Johann Sebastian Bach returned to Cöthen where he devoted himself above all to work on the *Well-Tempered Clavier,* his greatest work for keyboard in both its inward and its outward dimensions. Once again he directed his efforts to the "musical youth eager to learn" as well as to those "already perfected in this study"—that is, to both the student and the artist. It serves not only the keyboard player but also the composer with model compositions of unique quality and variety. Each of the twenty-four preludes and each of the companion fugues manifests a wholly novel and independent realization of its genre. Whether or not the designation "well-tempered" refers to the tuning of equal degrees that was coming into use at the time, for which Andreas Werckmeister had laid the theoretical groundwork in the late seventeenth century, still remains to be clarified. It is equally conceivable that Bach was still reckoning with a tuning or "temperament" that left to each tonality its individual character, its distinct tonal flavor. What is essential to the *Well-Tempered Clavier* is that here for the first time works of the highest quality were created for all twelve steps of the chromatic scale, in both the major and minor modes. This work, completed in 1722, was to be followed later by another identically ordered sequence of twenty-four preludes and fugues. Published in 1744, they became known as the *Well-Tempered Clavier,* Book Two.

In February 1721 news reached Bach from Ohrdruf of the death of his oldest brother Johann Christoph, with whom Bach had found shelter upon being orphaned at age ten. This news must have moved him with recollections of that earlier time, as now his own growing children were motherless. Were Bach to die, no "Johann Christoph" stood ready to receive the younger brothers and sisters, for Bach's oldest son, Wilhelm Friedemann, was only ten years old. For his own sake, too, Bach must have longed for a new companion. To be sure, his sadness over the early death of his beloved Maria Barbara was great; the memory of his wife cast a distinct shadow over his daily life, as only a bright light can do. But in time he decided it better to kindle a new light than to lament the darkness: "The purpose of life is life itself!" The creative man needed a quiet companion and trusted intimate who in love could transform his homeless round of activities into a familiar garden where he could live and work.

So on 3 December 1721 Bach married his second wife, the twenty-year-old Anna Magdalena Wilcken. As the youngest daughter of Johann Casper Wilcken, "Court and Field Trumpeter of the Music of His Highness the Prince of Saxe-Weissenfels," she had been trained as a soprano and had received an appointment as "Royal Singer" in the court ensemble of Prince Leopold of Anhalt-Cöthen. Anna Magdalena was able to restore the atmosphere of beauty and friendliness her husband so greatly needed for his well-being and his artistic creativity. She was a calm and graceful companion for her husband, always ready with help and encouragement, and a loving and cheerful mother to the children. Clearly she was one of those women whose very being graces with ease and comfort the innermost lives of those entrusted to her. In the presence of such a wife Bach was comforted in thinking of his death. He could die in peace, the children well provided for:

With thee beside, I go with joy
To death and to my last reposing.
O how glad would be my end,
The fingers of thy loving hand
My trusting eyelids gently closing.

Johann Sebastian included these lines in the "Little Clavier Book" he gave his wife in 1725, setting them to a simple melody. This "Little Clavier Book," together with an earlier one from 1722, gives happy testimony to the human and professional harmony that must have existed between Johann Sebastian and Anna Magdalena Bach. In this clavier book, besides sacred and secular songs and exercises and smaller compositions for clavier, we also find early drafts of the French Suites. Together with the six English Suites and the six partitas of later composition, they belong among the most significant documents of the art of the suite. Bach's wife took part in his great work. She helped him prepare copies, or wrote out choral and instrumental parts when necessary. In time her handwriting became so similar to her husband's that even Bach researchers have difficulty distinguishing the two.

Only a few reports concerning Anna Magdalena Bach have come down to us. One of them is a short note by Johann Elias Bach, a nephew of Johann Sebastian who lived in his house for a time as a foster son. He reports Anna Magdalena's joy over receiving six carnation plants: "She treasured this gift more highly than children do their Christmas presents, and tended them with such care as is usually given to small children, lest a single one wither." At another time Johann Elias reports her delight over a trained finch, a linnet. Anna Magdalena's full heart enjoyed the simplest pleasures life held in store for her. Small lights, not dazzling but dispelling of shadows, illumined her days.

Thirteen children were born to Bach and Anna Magdalena, of whom seven died in earliest childhood. Among the surviving sons were two who, like Wilhelm Friedemann and Carl Philipp Emanuel, were to become prominent composers: Johann Christoph Friedrich, who became known as the "Bückeburg Bach," and Johann Christian, who became famous in Milan and London as a composer of operas, symphonies, clavier concertos, and sonatas.

Very shortly after Bach's marriage on 3 December 1721 changes in the court at Cöthen once again necessitated a change of location for the master. On 11 December, Prince Leopold married Princess Friederica Henrietta of Anhalt-Bernburg, who at once had a detrimental influence on the court's musical life, formerly so luxuriant. Bach reported to Georg Erdmann: "One is resigned to the fact that the aforementioned Serenissimus has married a Princess of Berenburg and that thereupon the said Prince's musical inclination has become somewhat lukewarm, particularly since the new Princess appears to be an *a-musa*" (one untouched by the Muses).

We have already seen that after Maria Barbara's death Bach felt himself again drawn more strongly to church music. Nevertheless, he would scarcely have exchanged his post as court capellmeister for a church position without much deliberation. Besides the fact that in the enlightened eighteenth century a high-court position was more generally respected than a church position, it was also more satisfactory to be subject to a single prince than to be under a corporate consistory or city council. On the other hand, a court position could be genuinely satisfying for an artist only when the prince promoted artistic productivity with the attention and support appropriate to works of value. Where this was not the case a court post could be not only unsatisfying but also insecure, as the Berlin example of 1713 following the death of Frederick I had illustrated. With Leopold's marriage to the *"a-musa,"* the situation in Cöthen had changed

Friederica Henrietta,
princess of Anhalt-Cöthen.
Engraving by
J. C. G. Fritzsch, 1756.

for the worse. Thus Bach took special note when the death of Johann Kuhnau on 5 June 1722 left vacant the cantorship of the St. Thomas Church in Leipzig.

With a population of thirty thousand Leipzig was a large city for those days, offering a musician like Bach possibilities beyond those of the small residence city of Cöthen. Also, being most closely associated with orthodox Lutheranism, it was a prominent patron city of church music, and the cantor of St. Thomas bore general responsibility for the musical activities of all the churches of the city. What is more, Leipzig had a university at which Bach's sons might study. All of this finally led Bach to apply to the

View of Leipzig. Engraving by J. G. Ringlin, c. 1720.

Leipzig city council in December 1722 to succeed Johann Kuhnau as the St. Thomas cantor.

His chances seemed favorable when Georg Philipp Telemann, whom the council had in the meantime already selected, declined, having succeeded in obtaining more favorable working conditions in his Hamburg post. The Leipzigers still did not consider Bach the best candidate, however. Upon Telemann's refusal they sought the Darmstadt court capellmeister, Christoph Graupner. Only after he too had declined—his master, Count Ernst Ludwig of Hesse-Darmstadt, having declared himself prepared to increase Graupner's wages significantly so as to keep him in Darmstadt—did Bach receive the call to Leipzig. "As the best could not be obtained, we must take the middling": so state the Leipzig council minutes!

It should be mentioned to Christoph Graupner's credit that with his refusal he recommended that the Leipzig city council call Johann Sebastian Bach, whom he praised as "a musician as competent in organ playing as he is experienced in church affairs and orchestral repertory." Yet before the council was able to decide in favor of Bach, he had to present himself as a composer of sacred music. So between January and March 1723, Bach composed the *St. John Passion.* It was performed in the St. Thomas Church on Good Friday, 26 March. Still the city authorities were not satisfied. Bach was required to exhibit before the official selection proceedings a dismissal letter from the Prince of Anhalt-Cöthen. This condition, too, was met. Prince Leopold recommended his capellmeister:

Whereas We have at all times been well content with his discharge of his duties, but the said Bach, wishing now to seek his fortune elsewhere, has accordingly most humbly petitioned Us to grant him a most gracious dismissal, now therefore We have been pleased graciously to grant him the same and to give him highest recommendation for service elsewhere.

Finally, on 19 April, Bach had to promise the Leipzig city council solemnly that "if my request be granted and the said post be entrusted to me, I will within three or, at the most, four weeks from this date make myself free of the engagement given me at the Court of the Prince of Anhalt-Cöthen, and convey to the said Council the certificate of dismissal I receive."

Only when all these conditions had been fulfilled was Bach chosen on 22 April 1723. A month later, on 22 May, he and his family arrived in Leipzig. On 1 June, he was officially installed as the St. Thomas cantor. The last period of Johann Sebastian Bach's life had begun.

The St. Thomas Cantor

Johann Sebastian Bach remained in Leipzig for the rest of his life. For twenty-seven years he served as cantor of St. Thomas Church, and as the Thomas cantor he entered into history. In a letter Bach wrote on 28 October 1730 to his friend and former Lüneburg school companion Georg Erdmann we read:

At first, indeed, it did not seem at all proper to me to change my position of capellmeister for that of cantor. Wherefore, then, I postponed my decision for a quarter of a year; but this post was described to me in such favorable terms that finally (particularly since my sons seemed inclined toward [university] studies) I cast my lot, in the name of the Lord, and made the journey to Leipzig, took my examination, and then made the change of position. Here, by God's will, I am still in service.

Bach had decided in favor of Leipzig only with hesitation, and for a long time he continued cordial relations with Cöthen and Prince Leopold. Just before Bach's move to Leipzig, Princess Friederica Henrietta, the *"a-musa,"* had died, and Leopold's inclination for music had reasserted itself as vitally as before. During his first Leipzig years Bach traveled regularly to Cöthen to make music in the familiar settings or to perform festival cantatas for Leopold's birthday on 10 December. When Leopold married a music-loving princess in 1725, Bach wrote a birthday cantata for her as well. To the young prince who was born within a year's time Bach dedicated his harpsichord Partita in B minor, as well as a poem of homage he had authored himself.

On 19 November 1728, shortly before the completion of his thirty-fourth year of life, Prince Leopold died. Bach traveled to Cöthen for a final time. For the beloved prince's burial service he directed the finest and most beautiful funeral music ever to sound at a German prince's grave. Bach had provided new texts for several sections of his *St. Matthew Passion,* and with this funeral cantata he bade farewell to his princely friend.

The illustrations of the following pages:
30) Organ façade of the St. Thomas Church in Leipzig.
31) Johann Sebastian Bach. Painting by E. G. Haussmann.
32) The St. Thomas Church in Leipzig.
33) Interior of the St. Nicholas Church in Leipzig.
34) Council chamber of Leipzig's old city hall.
35) View of Dresden. Painting by Canaletto.
36) Elector August "the Strong."

This was Bach's last visit to Cöthen. Soon thereafter the musicians of the court orchestra were discharged. Cöthen, the place of origin for the Brandenburg Concertos and the Orchestral Suites, the *Well-Tempered Clavier* and the *St. John Passion,* had in musical terms ceased to exist.

The duties and tasks Bach had to fulfill in Leipzig were in sharp contrast with those of the royal court at Cöthen. That sacred vocal music now replaced the secular chamber music of the court was merely the most obvious difference. Of greater significance was the fact that in Cöthen an ensemble of prominent professional musicians had been at Bach's disposal, whereas in Leipzig music was performed largely by scholars, students, and town pipers, whose abilities were far below those of court musicians. They were in fact depressingly mediocre. What is more, instead of serving a young, cultivated, and music-loving prince, Bach was now accountable to an incalculable multitude of church and city notables, frequently at odds among themselves.

Added to all this were oppressive working conditions, stemming in part from the general historical structure of the cantor's post, but also relating to conditions in Leipzig's St. Thomas School that were particularly terrible at that time. In Cöthen, Bach had found sufficient time for composing outside his clearly delimited services to the court. In Leipzig, however, he had to wage wearisome battles for such time, since the cantorship left practically no leisure for creativity. For the former court singer Anna Magdalena Bach the move to Leipzig meant the end of her activities as a vocalist, since those times still allowed no opportunity for a woman to appear as a soloist in church. Bach made great sacrifices, then, to achieve his understandable desires of producing church music again and allowing his sons the advantages of a university city.

The Protestant cantorship was a creation of Martin Luther and his musical collaborator, Johann Walter, near the beginning of the sixteenth century. Luther loved music: "Youth should always be familiarized with this art, for it makes for fine and capable persons. I give *musica* the next place after *theologia,* and the highest honor." For Luther, music was intrinsic to education: "Whoever has no desire or love for it and is not moved by such lovely wonders must surely be an uncouth clod, who does not deserve to hear beautiful music!" In worship music appeared to him as an indispensable means for proclaiming the divine good tidings. Here he differed significantly from the representatives of the Swiss Reformation, Zwingli and Calvin, who perceived sensual danger in the arts.

For I am not of the opinion that all the arts should be struck down by the gospel and perish, as some spurious spiritualists would gladly see happen. Rather I would see all the arts, but especially music, in the service of Him who created and bestowed them.

Besides simple hymns for congregational singing, of which he himself wrote many, Luther most loved and marveled at the exalted art of polyphony. He fervently encouraged its nurture among the cantors of the larger churches. What especially filled him with astonishment was the so-called *Tenorsatz,* that is, the art of joining other contrapuntal voices to a given melody. Indeed, such art actually appeared to him as a proof of the divine origin and nature of music:

But where natural music is refined and polished by art, there one first sees and recognizes the great and perfect wisdom of God in his miraculous work of music. The most rare and marvelous musical creation of all occurs when a simple melody or *tenor* (as the musicians call it) is joined by three or four or five other voices, joyfully playing and skipping around it, decorating and adorning that simple, ordinary melody most wonderfully in various ways, with various sounds, as if in some heavenly roundelay of dance.

Such frankly ecstatic musical enthusiasm as Luthers's upon hearing polyphonic chorale motets had not been uttered since the *Confessions* of St. Augustine. With what joy would Luther have eavesdropped on the chorale cantatas created from his own melodies by Bach, two hundred years later!

In the Protestant church founded by Luther the cantor was obligated to teach the Latin school students subjects like Latin, rhetoric, and the catechism, as well as a broadly conceived course of musical instruction. The latter began with the singing of simple, unison chorale melodies (the *cantus planus*), and ended with the performance of complicated compositions *(cantus figuralis)* in the *chorus symphoniacus,* also known as the "first chorus" or, as in Lüneburg, the "matins choir." Instruction in music theory was also included.

Since the cantor had to teach academic in addition to musical subjects, the church or city authorities liked to employ a musician with a university education—a magister, if possible. The cantor was further expected to be capable of composing his own motets and cantatas for performance in the worship services. It is evident that with increasing musical obligations and demands the additional nonmusical duties would become more and more of a burden for the cantor, who would try to avoid them whenever possible. Naturally this would lead to dissension.

At the same time the cantor was obliged as music director, or *director musices,* to maintain supervision of the musical activities of all the city's churches and thus, as the authoritative figure, to determine the city's overall musical life. This included nonchurch occasions such as election festivals, royal receptions, family celebrations in patrician homes, and the like. From all these occasions requiring musical embellishment the cantor in his role as music director received additional perquisites, the so-called accidentals. Their amount was established by the city council, and as a rule they exceeded the basic salary many times over. Such payments were only for performances, not for composition of the works that made the performances possible.

If Johann Sebastian Bach was happier in Leipzig with the role of music director than with the role of cantor, this was first because the position of city music director corresponded more closely to that of capellmeister than did the position of cantor. Also, in the former role he could truly develop as an artist and as the city's leading musician, whereas as cantor he had to attend to a multitude of often menial distractions, from conducting wearisome singing lessons, or *Singstunden,* with undisciplined students, to serving every fourth week as school inspector, overseeing school discipline and supervising the students from five o'clock in the morning (six o'clock in winter) until eight o'clock at night. It is self-evident that during such weeks musical composition lay fallow.

Soon after commencing his new duties Bach was able to delegate at least the Latin instruction to a colleague, whom of course he then had to pay. Instruction in the Lutheran catechism, however, he conducted himself, and likewise the teaching of music theory. Needless to say he continued teaching gifted students, among them Johann Ludwig Krebs, Johann Philipp Kirnberger, Johann Friedrich Agricola, Christoph Nichelmann, his future son-in-law Johann Christoph Altnikol, and above all, his own sons, who later used to say with pride that they had had no teacher other than their father.

Occasional trips offered welcome changes (much to the displeasure of the church consistory), especially trips to foreign courts such as Dresden and Cassel, where Bach gave organ concerts and played with prominent musicians who in turn would visit him in Leipzig. Often he was invited to inspect or try out organs, for his reputation throughout Germany as an organ expert was as brilliant as his fame as an organ virtuoso. Indeed, not only in Germany. In a letter written on 14 April 1750 by the important music theorist and composer Padre Giambattista Martini of Bologna we read:

I feel it would be superfluous to go further into the unique merits of Signor Bach, for he is very well known and admired not only in Germany but in all of Italy as well. I shall say only that I would consider it difficult to find a musician to surpass him; for he can justly pride himself on being one of the first in Europe today.

The realities of the living conditions in Leipzig under which Bach was constrained to work stand in stark opposition to this declaration by Padre Martini. When his situation became particularly unbearable, he once again tried to find a change of location. He pleaded for help, in vain, to his friend Erdmann:

I find that the post is by no means so lucrative as it had been described to me; I have failed to obtain many of the fees pertaining to the office; the place is very expensive; and the authorities are odd and little interested in music, so that I must live amid almost continual vexation, envy, and persecution; accordingly I shall be forced, with God's help, to seek my fortune elsewhere.

This wish, however, came to nothing. Bach remained in Leipzig until his death.

What were Bach's obligations at St. Thomas? After Bach had been selected as cantor by the council and consistory on 22 April 1723, he had to sign an official document on 5 May in which he solemnly vowed "to give due obedience to the Honorable Inspectors and Directors of the School in each and every instruction which the same shall issue in the name of the Honorable and Most Wise Council," and also "through honorable life and conduct to set a good example for the youths." Afterward Bach returned to Cöthen to prepare for his transfer and to see to the moving of his family.

The arrival of the Bach family in Leipzig on 22 May 1723 received mention in the newspaper:

Last Saturday around noon four wagons arrived from Cöthen loaded with household goods belonging to the former royal capellmeister, now come to Leipzig as *cantor figuralis.* Around two o'clock he himself arrived, together with his family in two coaches, whom he deposited in the newly renovated residence of the St. Thomas School.

(The title used here, *cantor figuralis,* relates to the motets and cantatas set in the style of *cantus figuralis* or polyphony, the composition and performance of which were among the most important obligations of the cantor, as contrasted with those of the organist.)

The St. Thomas School was located alongside the St. Thomas Church in a building dating from 1553. Besides the teachers and their families it housed some fifty-five boarding students *(Alumnen)*—students from poor homes who had been granted free positions in the boarding school on the basis of their good singing voices alone. In return they were obliged to take part in the music of worship services, and more particularly to be available at any time music was needed for a wedding, a funeral, or a public festival. To obtain further alms they had to sing in the streets, even in winter—at St. Martin's Day in November, for example, or at the feast of Epiphany in January. Many of these children were ill or neglected. Sanitary conditions in the St. Thomas School must have been appalling at times. We read in a report of 1728:

Thirst was unbearable (especially in the hot days of summer). Further, it afflicted many poor children who, having no means of support from home, often had to climb over the water urn that stood in the chamber and drink in common with the rats (which at that time were present in frightful numbers). The poor boys had to endure a great deal.

Thus, St. Thomas School in 1728.

In this same house and at this same time the *St. Matthew Passion* was written! Bach's residence was separated from the students' sleeping quarters by only a thin wall. Not every student had his own bed. The lack of space in the house was a calamity. Of the thirteen of Bach's children who were born here, no fewer than seven died in earliest childhood, and the unimaginable sanitary conditions of the school building must surely have been partly to blame. In response to these conditions the city authorities simply regulated the daily schedule more rigorously. The house regulations, newly formulated in the year Bach's service began, state:

As soon as the bell rings—at five o'clock in the summer, six o'clock in the winter—each student must arise, wash, comb, and within a quarter of an hour be ready to come down for prayers, bringing his Bible. Clothes, shoes, stockings, and linen must be kept clean. ... Before the time of retiring, the day's lessons must be recited and the Most High thanked for what has been learned. ... Before and after the midday and evening meals the youth whose turn it is will say grace and the others will repeat it after him. During the meal a Psalm or a chapter from the Bible or from some other edifying book shall be read aloud.

Leipzig was a long way from Cöthen!

If in retrospect we survey the workload Bach had to bear in his roles as cantor and music director, it appears to us an inexplicable miracle that in the midst of all this he was still able to create so colossal an artistic corpus. He was responsible for the musical arrangements for worship in all five of Leipzig's churches. Besides the two main churches, St. Thomas and St. Nicholas, there were St. Peter's, the New Church, and St. Paul's, belonging to the university. In the two main churches a four-hour worship service was held each Sunday, in the course of which performances of both a motet and a cantata were required, and the cantatas had to be composed beforehand. Altogether Bach may have composed, rehearsed, and performed close to three hundred cantatas, many of which are now lost.

The high holy days of Christmas and Easter brought additional and extraordinary demands. On the twenty-fourth, twenty-fifth, and twenty-sixth of December, on Good Friday, and on both the Easter feast days, *two* worship services required music. Bach set himself the task of producing works of his own for all these services. For his first Christmas in Leipzig Bach composed, in addition to a series of cantatas, the splendid *Magnificat,* Mary's song of praise from Luke's Gospel. The ensuing years produced the motets, the *St. Matthew Passion,* the *Christmas Oratorio,* the B-Minor Mass, the organ sonatas—all these unique masterpieces despite a harassing daily routine of conducting chorallessons, supervising troops of undisciplined students, copying music, procuring materials, holding choir auditions (usually with wholly insufficient performers), negotiating with town piper unions, and finally holding up through the many and lengthy services of worship.

Yet Bach could scarcely have supported his large family if he had restricted his activities merely to the duties just named. They brought him a basic salary of only one hundred talers—only slightly more than he had received in Arnstadt—together with a fixed allowance for firewood, wax candles, and grain, and two tankards of wine at Easter, Whitsuntide, and Christmas. Thus he was forced to secure additional income. With the help of these "accidentals" he could attain a yearly income of about seven hundred talers. But it meant that beyond his many duties as cantor he had to be constantly on the move attending all sorts of festivals, weddings, baptisms, burials, town hall celebrations, university occasions, and processions in honor of some visiting dignitary, in order to perform with choirs and town piper ensembles. The requisite music had to be composed, vocal and instrumental parts prepared, and rehearsals conducted. Yet still these years produced one masterpiece after another.

In view of such a life, who would wonder that Bach sometimes neglected one or another choral lesson, this or that catechism session? His superiors, however, knew no forbearance. In a council session of 2 August 1730 a certain Councillor Steger entered this opinion into the minutes: "Not only does the cantor do nothing, but he was not even willing to give an explanation of that fact; he is not holding the singing lessons and there are other complaints in addition; a change would be necessary." The council consequently passed a resolution "to reduce the cantor's wages, as he is incorrigible." This salary reduction went into effect on 6 November 1730. To the hostile and unappreciative conduct of the city council was added unrelenting hatefulness on the part of superior authorities at the St. Thomas School. After 1734 a rector by the name of Johann August Ernesti was especially zealous in attempting to minimize the importance of musical education in favor of subjects in the natural sciences.

But let us return once more to the particular musical conditions under which Bach had to work in Leipzig. Normally only eight instrumentalists were available to him for performances of his cantatas and other choral works, namely, four town pipers, three professional fiddlers, and one journeyman town piper. "Discretion forbids me from speaking truth about their qualities and musical knowledge"—such was Bach's judgment of this miniature orchestra. Matters were scarcely better with the choir responsible for performances of cantatas and motets, the *chorus symphoniacus*. This is the obvious conclusion from an urgent memorandum Bach directed to the city council on 23 August 1730 in which he appealed for an increase in the funds designated for musical performances. The heading reads: "A Short but Most Necessary Draft for Well-

St. Thomas churchyard with church and school. Lithograph (1732) by C. C. Böhme.

Appointed Church Music; with Certain Modest Reflections on the Decline of the Same." Then Bach described to the authorities in specific detail what a halfway tolerable performance corps would look like. He claimed that each choir part should consist of at least three and preferably four singers. Ideally, then, he envisioned a choir of sixteen voices (quite small by today's standards). In the orchestra he wanted sometimes two to three players for the first and second violin parts; likewise two players for the viola and violoncello parts, and one for contrabass; three oboists; possibly also two flutists, two bassoonists, three trumpeters, and one tympanist—altogether some twenty to twenty-two instrumentalists. Although today this seems a minimal ensemble, Bach's memorandum found no hearing among the council.

If after 1729 Bach was nevertheless able on occasion to perform works with the forces here enumerated, this was thanks to the free and voluntary participation of student musical enthusiasts of Leipzig University. Without the willing help of students a work like the *St. Matthew Passion,* first heard on Good Friday 1729, could not have been performed. In that same year Bach had taken over the university's *Collegium Musicum,* founded in 1702 by Georg Philipp Telemann. Originally its twenty or so members had made music without pay in Zimmermann's Coffeehouse, performing secular cantatas and instrumental chamber music. Though Bach's relationship with the university leadership was not exactly a happy one, still he always found students who were glad to stand up for him and his music, and on whom he could count for collaboration in church performances as well. This *Collegium Musicum* alone made Bach's transfer from Cöthen to Leipzig rewarding, and without this youthful ensemble a work like the *St. Matthew Passion* would have remained unperformed, perhaps even unwritten.

As the city council did not even take cognizance of this miraculous work, so too it was unprepared to support a second performance Bach had planned for 27 March 1739. Thus a century had to pass before this work was heard again on 11 March 1829 under the direction of Felix Mendelssohn Bartholdy. Since then Bach's great confessional work, the *St. Matthew Passion,* has become the universal possession of humankind. All who are prepared to let themselves be gripped by this work and to open themselves to its message have the right to experience this music in their own wholly personal ways. An introduction to such a work from an analytic or "passion-history" point of view would hinder more than benefit. More eloquent, rather, are the words of the philosopher Friedrich Nietzsche upon hearing Bach's *St. Matthew Passion* in 1870: "One who has completely forgotten Christianity truly hears it here as gospel."

The illustrations of the following pages:
37) Page from the score of the *St. Matthew Passion.*
38) Frederick the Great.
39) Music salon in Sans Souci Palace.
40) Pages from the score of the *Art of the Fugue.*
41) J. S. Bach in old age.
    The sons:
42) Carl Philipp Emanuel, 43) Wilhelm Friedemann,
44) Johann Christoph Friedrich, 45) Johann Christian.
46) Johann Sebastian Bach's grave marker in the St. Thomas Church.

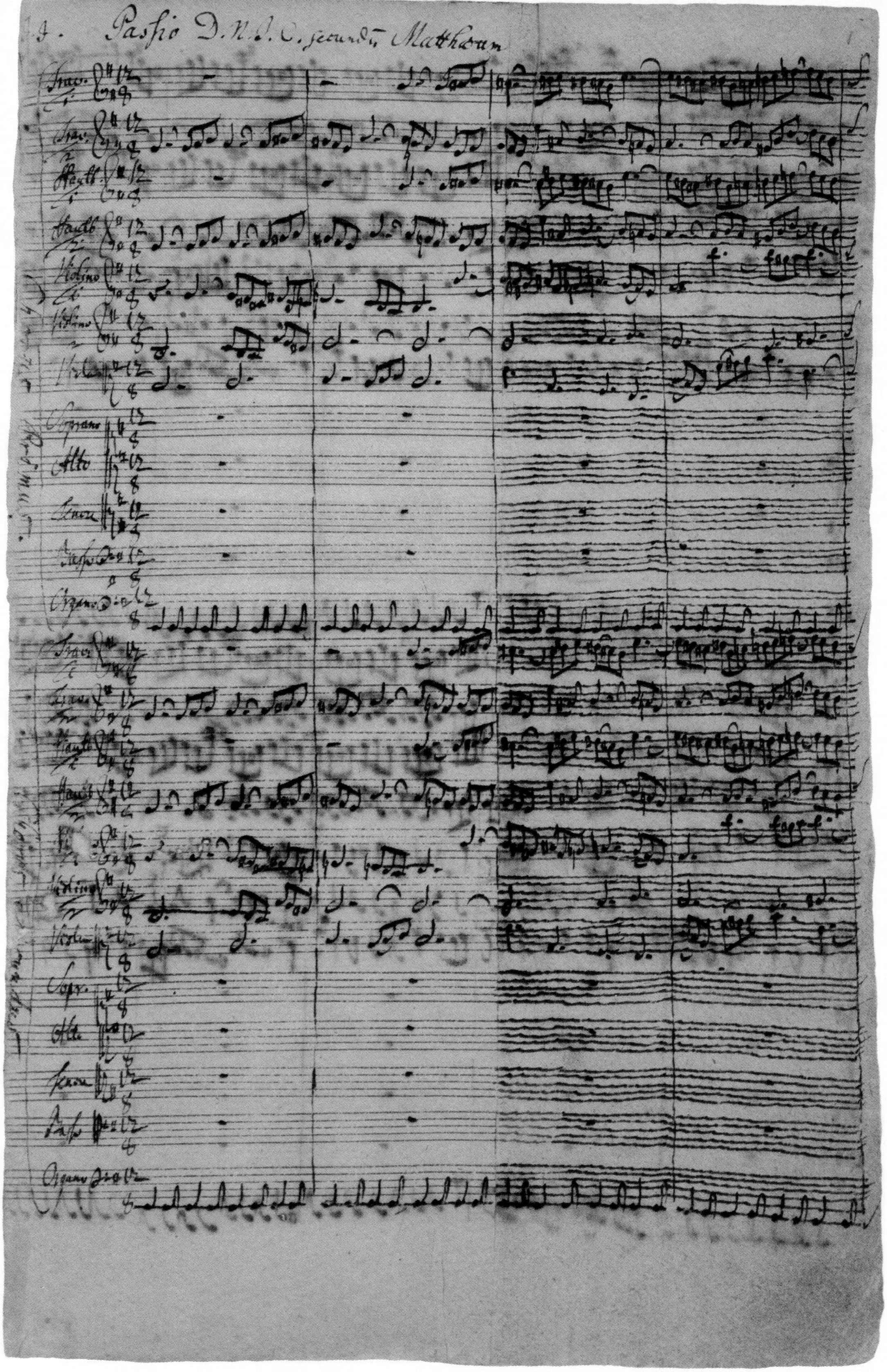
Passio D.N.J.C. secundum Matthaeum
Soprano
Alto
Tenore
Basso
Organo

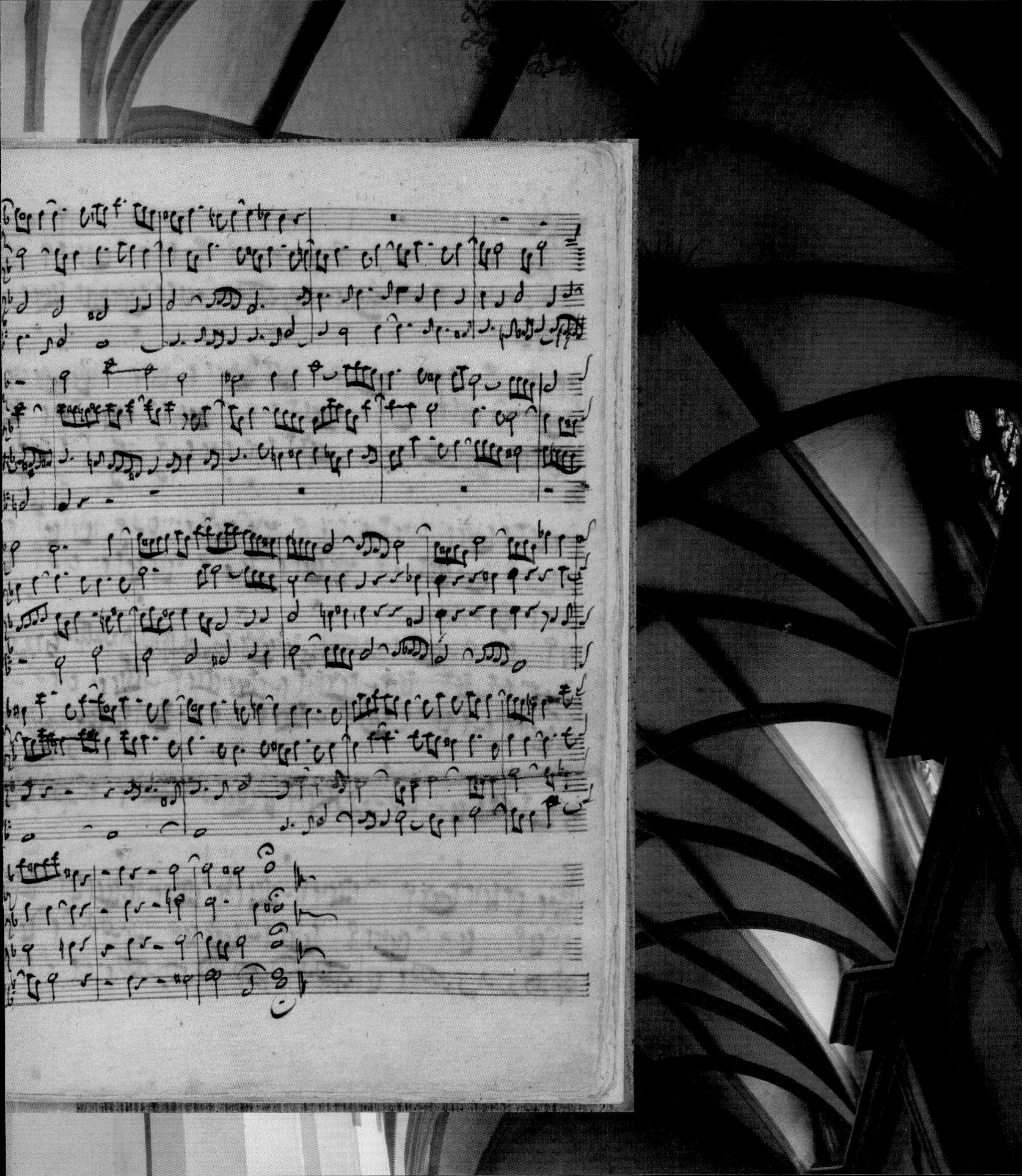

A year after the performance of the *St. Matthew Passion* on 15 April 1729 relations between the St. Thomas cantor and his governing authorities had reached such an unendurable state that, as we have already seen, Bach was of a mind to leave Leipzig. That such a move never eventuated may be attributed principally to the fact that at just this time Johann Matthias Gesner, the highly cultured and music-loving classical philologist, was entrusted with the leadership of St. Thomas School as its new rector. With Gesner the cantor's life at once improved notably. Two new stories were added to the school building, so that the urgent need for space could be remedied. Also, Gesner saw to it that Bach was largely freed from his many time-consuming, nonmusical obligations.

Of particular significance was Gesner's attitude toward music. Convinced of music's power to cultivate character, he restored this subject to an important place in the curriculum, whereby he also enhanced respect for Bach among his colleagues. Gesner's understanding of music was oriented less to the Lutheran concept of music as *laudatio Dei* than to the humanistic teachings of Plato and Aristotle. According to them, music's most distinctive function is to ensure a cultivated form of health for body and soul. For Gesner, a deep, intentional engagement with music guaranteed a noble and free mode of life, of the kind believed by classical antiquity and again later during the Italian Renaissance to befit the nature of a free person.

Unfortunately, after only four years Gesner left Leipzig for a professorship at the University of Göttingen. Even from there, however, he thought of his friend Johann Sebastian Bach. Specifically, as he was writing a scholarly commentary on the *Institutio Oratoria*, the famous study of rhetoric by Fabius Quintilian (first century A. D.), he introduced Bach into his work in a most perceptive way, as original as it was adroit. Gesner comments upon Quintilian's laudatory mention of a virtuoso Greek cithara player with the following words:

You would think but slightly, my dear Fabius (Quintilianus), of all these . . . , if, returning from the underworld, you could see Bach . . . , either playing our clavier which is many citharas in one, with all the fingers of both hands, or running over the keys of the instrument of instruments, whose innumerable pipes are brought to life by bellows, with both hands and, at the utmost speed, with his feet, producing by himself the most various and at the same time mutually agreeable combinations of sounds in orderly procession. If you could see him, I say, . . . not only, like a citharoedist, singing with one voice . . . but watching over everything and bringing back to the rhythm and the beat, out of thirty or even forty musicians, the one with a nod, another by tapping with his foot, the third with a warning finger, . . . all alone, in the midst of the greatest din made by all the participants, . . . noticing at once whenever and wherever a mistake occurs, holding everyone together, taking precautions everywhere, and repairing any unsteadiness, full of rhythm in every part of his body—this one man taking in all these harmonies with his keen ear and emitting with his voice alone the tone of all the voices. Favorer as I am of antiquity, the accomplishments of our Bach, and of any others that there may be like him, appear to me to effect what not many Orpheuses, nor twenty Arions, could achieve.

This remembrance of a Bach rehearsal is so vivid as to suggest that Johann Matthias Gesner may have collaborated as an active participant while in his Leipzig rector's post.

After Gesner's departure from Leipzig, he was succeeded on 16 November 1734 by Johann August Ernesti as director of the St. Thomas School at only twenty-seven years of age. Ernesti was thoroughly acquainted with the affairs of the school, as his father Johann Heinrich had been rector earlier and he himself had held the post of deputy rector up until Gesner's leaving. At first it appeared that Bach might be able to live in agreement with his new superior. In 1736, however, something happened—of little significance in itself—that led to two years of strife and was finally carried to the elector of Saxony, still with no satisfactory resolution. The conflict had to do with the question of whether the rector or the cantor had the right to appoint the choir prefects. Hidden behind this problem, at first glance so seemingly insignificant, was a tradition of great religious and historical importance.

From a legal point of view the cantor had undoubtedly always had the right to appoint the prefects. If Ernesti nevertheless claimed this right for himself, he did so because he called into question the very post of cantor itself. This post in Martin Luther's sense presupposed for its legitimation an undiminished acknowledgment of the old, theocentric world view. Precisely this, however, Ernesti was unwilling to grant, having been brought up in enlightened ways of thinking. Consequently he contested the cantor's traditional rights.

The eighteenth century has been called "the middle century," for in the course of this century European intellectual life underwent a process of fundamental revaluation. The theocentric, monistic world view inherited from the Middle Ages was loosened and an anthropocentric, pluralistic intellectual attitude was put in its place, in which humanity's existential state was then grounded. For those of the early eighteenth century—and here Bach throughout his life belonged—God still stood at the center of things. All was accomplished by him; in him all was secure. From about 1730 on, however, this submissiveness to God was increasingly called into question and finally broken under the influence of French and English Enlightenment philosophy, whereby traditional ecclesiastical and theological systems of thought were abandoned in favor of a modern view and understanding of the world. This new world view no longer grounded itself in incontrovertible truths of faith but rather in the principles of *ratio,* *sensus,* and *empirie* first proven in the realm of the natural sciences. That is, it grounded

106

itself in knowledge acquired with the help of human understanding, sense perception, and practical experience. Within this world view adherents of the Enlightenment believed they could attain human happiness, not simply in the hereafter but before—specifically, here on earth. The acknowledged means to this end was an education grounded in reason and "virtue" in the sense of a free humanity. Ushering in an ennobled humanity by these means was the lofty goal of enlightened pedagogues in the mid-eighteenth century. Such was the goal of Johann August Ernesti.

This fundamental alteration in the general understanding of world and existence had profound consequences for the understanding of music as well. The conception of music and its aims changed in the course of the eighteenth century no less radically than the more general revaluation we have just depicted. Music's aim was no longer the praise of God but rather the delighting of the ear and the stirring of the heart.

Johann Sebastian Bach may have felt at a disadvantage in that he could not enter the conflict looming before him with the same weapons as those available to his antagonists. He had sunk the roots of his intellectual and spiritual existence firmly in old soil. There he had found support, and this was the soil that would provide his support—unshakable support—from now on. He sank his roots deeper and deeper into that trusted soil. Bedrock itself would grant him additional strength and make him unconquerable:

Yea, though I walk through the valley of the shadow of death, I will fear no evil: for thou art with me; thy rod and thy staff they comfort me. . . . Surely goodness and mercy shall follow me all the days of my life: and I will dwell in the house of the Lord forever.

Bach's steadfast faith would remain unmolested "though the earth be removed, and though the mountains be carried into the midst of the sea; though the waters thereof roar and be troubled, though the mountains shake with the swelling thereof." The psalmist's convictions were Bach's as well.

In his inner life Bach now became progressively more solitary, notwithstanding his large family and the many friends and foreign colleagues who eagerly sought out the unfailing hospitality of his home. Bach turned to the realms that seemed to him to represent continuations of his old and trusted world. One such realm for Bach was still that of the elector of Saxony, the secular ruler whom Bach continued to view as the earthly counsel of a divinely established order. He was as ready and glad as ever to present a festive piece of homage to any prince who visited the city. Indeed, even the first part of the B-Minor Mass was composed and performed on the occasion of a visit to Leipzig by the elector. On that 21 April 1733 Elector Friedrich August II, son of August "the Strong," had appeared in Leipzig to receive the city's oath of fealty after the death of his father. Even the eleven-year-old elector prince, Friedrich Christian, was honored with a homage cantata composed especially for him. In the Leipzig press of 4 September 1733 the following announcement appeared:

The Bach *Collegium Musicum* will most humbly commemorate the exalted birthday of His Highness the Elector Prince of Saxony with a celebrative musicale on 5 September in the Zimmermann Garden before the Grimm Gate from four to six o'clock in the afternoon.

On another occasion, 2 October 1734, the elector appeared in Leipzig without warning. Bach had only three days to compose and rehearse a cantata. The students wanted to pay splendid homage to their sovereign on 5 October, the date on which in the previous year the elector had been chosen king of Poland. The Leipzig city chronicle reported:

Toward nine o'clock in the evening local students presented His Majesty with a most humble evening concert with trumpets and drums, composed by Capellmeister Johann Sebastian Bach, cantor of St. Thomas. Six hundred students all carried torches, and four counts, acting as marshals, played the music. The procession began at the bulletin board and progressed through Ritter, Brühl, and Catherine streets to the King's lodgings. As the music reached the public scales it was joined by trumpets and drums, likewise by a choir from the city hall. Upon presenting the poem, the four counts were allowed a kiss of the hand. His Royal Majesty, together with Her Royal Majesty and the Royal Prince, did not leave the window as long as the music continued, but graciously listened throughout. His Majesty was sincerely well pleased.

Bach had to prepare cantatas for secular festival days no fewer than fifty-three times. Many of these compositions he later provided with new texts, usually sacred, so that he was able to use them again. Many sections of the *Christmas Oratorio* (1734-35) trace back to secular cantatas. When in 1736 Bach was finally granted the title he much desired, "Compositeur of the Royal Polish and Elector of Saxony's Court," he savored this honor as an antidote to the insults inflicted upon him by the Leipzig authorities. The city council continued to see in him only the incorrigible school cantor, not the great musician, still less the superlative genius.

The primary sphere of Bach's life, proven and trusted, was his family. Bach found the personal and artistic strengths he needed at Anna Magdalena's side, surrounded by the children. The circle of those nearest to him was a secure barrier shielding him from the conflicts of everyday life. Like music, his family was for him an earthly manifestation of a good order. There he found a paradise from which there could be no expulsion. For his work he withdrew to his little "composing chamber," though much that issued from there could be tried out immediately in the family: "But they are all born musicians, and I can assure you that I can already form an ensemble both *vocaliter* and *instrumentaliter* within my family, particularly since my present wife sings a good, clear soprano, and my eldest daughter, too, joins in not badly." So we read in the letter, already quoted several times, that Bach wrote to his friend Georg Erdmann in 1730, at a time when Leipzig's city council was especially antagonistic toward him. No fewer than nineteen valuable musical instruments—claviers and stringed instruments of the most varied sorts, including a lute—are listed in the estate inventory drawn up in late autumn of 1750, several months after Bach's death. We can imagine the zeal of music making in the Bach family!

Bach must have followed the artistic progress of his sons with watchful pleasure and certainly with pride. He had already smoothed the first steps of their professional careers, for his word counted for a great deal in the musical world. Once they left home, however, he allowed them complete freedom in artistic matters, particularly as developing composers. It was therefore possible for them to experiment with new styles—each in his own way, and sometimes with fascinating boldness—and to attain new goals that made possible and indeed inaugurated a completely altered artistic reality, namely, that of the classical-romantic era. The alteration of musical style that took place between the baroque and Viennese classicism appears to us in retrospect as virtually a Bach family affair.

Wilhelm Friedemann, born in Weimar in 1710, was Sebastian's favorite and the object of his constant attention. With this constant solicitude, however, Bach may have unwittingly laid a basis for the many hardships that were to befall Friedemann after his father's death. Torn between the overpowering example of his father and the stylistic demands of changed times, he became the truly tragic figure in the family. Friedemann mastered organ performance and the baroque musician's compositional craft as only a few of his contemporaries were able to do. At the same time, however, he was filled with the impulses of a gifted, enlightened man, and for their realization these impulses required other means than those offered by his father's legacy. This ambiguity marked not only his work but also his life. Restless, without steady employment, shunned by his brothers, he shuttled from city to city. Halle, Leipzig, Berlin, Braunschweig, and Göttingen were his stations, usually only for short durations, until in 1784—completely impoverished—he died in Berlin. Friedemann was the only one of Johann Sebastian's sons who dared to live as a free artist, not bound by official courtly, ecclesiastical, or municipal duties. But the times were not yet full, and so he was bound to run aground.

Carl Philipp Emanuel, born in Weimar in 1714, was in comparison with Friedemann of a decidedly happy nature. No less gifted than his older brother, he had a healthy sense of humor and an inclination to sociability. He also had at his disposal a distinct talent for organization that always kept his feet firmly on the ground. As a law student in Frankfurt-on-the-Oder he already pursued what amounted to a public musical career. Soon thereafter he received a call from the Prussian crown prince Frederick to come to Rheinsberg, where he became chamber harpsichordist in the prince's orchestra. In this capacity he followed his sovereign to Berlin after the prince's accession to the throne as King Frederick II in 1740. Emanuel, whose compositions soon became widely known, also formed the center of the Berlin literary circle, which included the poets Lessing, Ramler, and Gleim, among others. Later, in 1768, Philipp Emanuel was called to Hamburg as music director and cantor. There he died in 1788, widely held in high esteem. His compositions made the most important contributions to the so-called *empfindsamer* style, a quiet, intimate music that appealed to people of that time, especially to the most discerning, as best suited to promote inspiration of mind and consonance of soul. It promoted the harmony between performer and listener that Goethe, too, always deemed an ideal much to be desired.

Johann Christoph Friedrich was born in Leipzig in 1732. In the year of his father's death he found a position as harpsichordist at the court of Count Wilhelm of Schaumburg-Lippe in Bückeburg, where he maintained allegiance throughout his life. In 1756 he became court capellmeister. During the period of Johann Gottfried Herder's presence in Bückeburg between 1771 and 1776 he made *empfindsamer* oratorio and cantata settings of Herder's texts. Later he adopted his younger brother's early classical style of writing, especially in his clavier sonatas, chamber works, and symphonies. Friedrich Bach died in Bückeburg in 1795.

Johann Christian, born in Leipzig in 1735, was the youngest son of Johann Sebastian Bach and also the son who most completely distanced himself from his father's model as a composer. He early became acquainted with Italian opera in Berlin. There, perhaps, his wish awakened to study this art at its source. In 1756 he went to Milan and soon thereafter to Bologna where he became a student of the famous Padre Martini. He converted to Catholicism and became organist at the Milan cathedral. He wrote operas for Turin and Naples and finally went to London in 1762. There in 1764 he met the eight-year-old Mozart, with whom he immediately formed a friendship. Christian was charmed by this child genius, and Mozart later recalled with gratitude the stimulation he had received from Christian Bach. Here Mozart first encountered Christian's style of music, glowing with Neapolitan cheerfulness, and today we know how important this artistic contact was for Mozart's future creativity. Johann Christian Bach died in London on New Year's Day 1782, the first of the well-known sons of Johann Sebastian Bach to die, despite the fact that he was also the youngest.

New musical paths, such as those followed by these sons, were no longer accessible to the father. Even though he remained an attentive observer of contemporary developments to the end, what he saw could not serve him as models. Thus he concerned himself not with fashionable stylizing of sound, but instead with spiritualizing his musical language within the style developed during the century before him—the style that perhaps would end with him, to which he must have known he was the last witness—namely, the style of polyphony. His B-Minor Mass, for example, strikes us more as a surpassing example of sacred art developed over more than half a millennium than as a work of the year 1733. If we recall that in that year Pergolesi's opera buffa "La serva padrona" appeared, we become especially aware of Bach's historical place as a "last witness."

With Bach's increasing inner isolation, another tendency began to manifest itself as well. After about 1735 he began to become aware of his historical mission and to understand this mission as imposing tasks he still had to fulfill. Thus the great, solitary figure, comparable to a Thomas Aquinas, created with his magnificent late works a *Summa Musicae* to bequeath to the future. He strove to gather, complete, and preserve his works. He produced the final settings of the Passions. In 1744 a sequence of twenty-four preludes and fugues formed a second collection after the pattern of the *Well-Tempered Clavier.* Six chorale settings from cantatas were adapted as organ chorales.

In addition, Bach now began to have works printed. In the four sections of the "Keyboard Exercise" *(Clavier-Übung)* he published the six partitas, the Italian Concerto, the French Overture in B minor, the chorale preludes "on the catechism and other songs," and the "aria with diverse variations for clavicimbal with two manuals" that we know by the name Goldberg Variations. This climactic example of the variation form (and of clavier music in general) is itself a *Summa Musicae.* A cycle of thirty variations upon a ground bass, it is arranged symmetrically according to an overall scheme and includes almost every conceivable variation possibility. It contains dance forms, virtuosic displays, and contrapuntal constructions of the greatest perfection, united in a self-contained exhibition of virtually encyclopedic scope. Finally, in 1746 Bach's "Canonical Variations on the Christmas Chorale 'From Heaven Above'" appeared, the *opus summum* of the chorale partita genre.

The year 1747 produced a notable experience for Johann Sebastian Bach. The Russian envoy to the Prussian court, Count Hermann Carl von Keyserlingk, for whom Bach had composed the Goldberg Variations, arranged an audience for the St. Thomas cantor with King Frederick the Great. The meeting, which was to give rise to the *Musical Offering,* took place on 7 May 1747 in the Potsdam palace. It is verified in four documentary accounts. Four days after the event the following report appeared in the *Berlin News* of 11 May:

We hear from Potsdam that last Sunday [May 7] the famous capellmeister from Leipzig, Mr. Bach, arrived with the intention of hearing the excellent Royal music at that place. In the evening, at about the time when the regular chamber music in the Royal apartments usually begins, His Majesty was informed that Capellmeister Bach had arrived at Potsdam and was waiting in His Majesty's antechamber for His Majesty's most gracious permission to listen to the music. His August Self immediately gave orders that Bach be admitted, and went, at his entrance, to the so-called "forte and piano," condescending also to play, in person and without any preparation, a theme to be executed by Capellmeister Bach in a fugue. This was done so happily by the aforementioned capellmeister that not only His Majesty was pleased to show his satisfaction thereat, but also all those present were seized with astonishment.

After returning to Leipzig Bach developed the royal theme into a great canonical work and dedicated it to the king as the *Musical Offering.*

Bach's life was coming to its close. The master focused his strength one final time into a huge work. The result was the *Art of the Fugue,* that all-surpassing culmination of Western counterpoint. Here fugal art is plumbed to its final possibilities, from simple, "normal" fugues at the beginning to the most complicated of constructions. But the work remained unfinished. After measure two hundred thirty-nine of the eighteenth fugue, a four-part fugue, the manuscript breaks off abruptly.

Bach became seriously ill in 1749, and his long-familiar tendency to nearsightedness had finally become blindness. The Leipzig city council acted promptly, in its inimitable fashion. On 8 June it had the Dresden conductor Johann Gottlob Harrer audition "for the future appointment as cantor of St. Thomas, in case capellmeister and cantor Mr. Sebastian Bach should die." But the blind Johann Sebastian Bach had not yet given up. His powerful spirit still wished to communicate. In a darkened room he dictated to the pen of his son-in-law Johann Christoph Altnikol his last ideas, note for note, line for line.

> The night shines deeper, to penetrate more deeply,
> But yet within there glows bright light.

Like the blind Faust, Bach hastened to bring his thoughts to fulfillment:

> For completing of the greatest work,
> One soul for a thousand hands suffices.

As Bach sensed that his death was imminent he dictated to Altnikol one final composition, the organ chorale "Before Thy Throne Herewith I Come." On 18 July 1750 he suffered a stroke from which he never recovered. After ten days, on 28 July, "a little after a quarter to nine in the evening, in the sixty-sixth year of his life, he quietly and peacefully, by the merit of his Redeemer, departed this life," as his obituary expressed it.

Anna Magdalena and the children were beside him when he died. Three of the children were still minors, and Anna Magdalena, who had no income of her own, had to petition the city council to grant her a "half year of grace," by which was meant a six-months' continuation of the wages her deceased husband had been receiving at the time of his death. Once again the Leipzig council remained true to its character. It reduced the widow's pension to exactly twenty-one talers and twenty-one groschen. The reason given was that when her husband had been named St. Thomas cantor twenty-seven years before, he had been paid for the entire first quarter but had begun his duties four weeks late. The council acted, as always, on the only basis it was capable of comprehending.

Ten years later, on 27 February 1760, Anna Magdalena died, utterly impoverished and forgotten—an "almswife" as the Leipzig funeral register coldly notes. No St. Thomas voices sang at her burial. She found her last resting place by the side of Johann Sebastian.

Johann Sebastian Bach's seal.

CHRONOLOGICAL TABLE

relating to the life and works of Johann Sebastian Bach

1685   21 March: Johann Sebastian Bach born in Eisenach (in the same year both George Frederick Handel and Domenico Scarlatti were born)

1687   Death of French composer Jean-Baptiste Lully

1689   First performance of Henry Purcell's opera *Dido and Aeneas*

1693-1695   Bach attends the Latin school in Eisenach; member of the school choir; instructed in violin by his father, Johann Ambrosius Bach

1694   Founding of the University of Halle (center of Pietism). 3 May: Death of Bach's mother, Elisabeth, née Lämmerhirt

1695   31 January: Death of Bach's father, Johann Ambrosius. Johann Sebastian and his brother Johann Jakob find shelter until 1700 in the house of their oldest brother, Johann Christoph, in Ohrdruf; Bach attends the gymnasium there; takes piano instruction with his brother, organ and violin instruction with the school cantors

1699   Founding of the Academy of Sciences in Berlin by Gottfried Wilhelm Leibniz

1700-1721   The Great Northern War (Charles XII of Sweden)

1700-1702   Bach attends the St. Michael's School in Lüneburg as a scholarship student or *Freischüler;* member (and later prefect) of the matins choir; contact with the organist Georg Böhm; trips to Hamburg (Jan Adams Reinken) and Celle (French organ and chamber music)

1701-1714   War of the Spanish Succession

1702   Georg Philipp Telemann as a student founds the *Collegium Musicum* at the University of Leipzig

1703   March to September(?): Bach serves as a violinist in the orchestra of Duke Johann Ernst of Saxe-Weimar

1703-1707   Organist at the St. Boniface Church in Arnstadt (installation on 9 August). 1704: "Capriccio sopra la lontananza del suo fratello diletissimo" (BWV 992). 1705-6: Four-month visit to Dietrich Buxtehude in Lübeck. 1705: Handel's first opera, "Almire," first performed in Hamburg. 1706: Jean-Philippe Rameau's "Le 1er livre des Pièces de clavecin"; Johann Pachelbel dies in Nürnberg; Johann August Böttger establishes a porcelain factory in Meissen near Dresden

1707-1708   Bach as organist at the St. Blasius Church in Mühlhausen (installation on 15 June 1707). 17 October 1707: Marriage with Barbara Bach in Dornheim. First preserved organ works and church cantatas (including "God's Time Is the Best of Times," also known as the "Actus Tragicus" [BWV 106])

1708-1717 July 1708: Bach called as chamber musician and court organist to the court of the reigning Duke Wilhelm Ernst of Saxe-Weimar; friendship with Johann Gottfried Walther and Georg Philipp Telemann; study of Italian music. 22 November 1710: Birth of son Wilhelm Friedemann. 2 March 1714: Named as concertmeister. 8 March 1714: Birth of son Carl Philipp Emanuel. In Weimar composition of great organ and clavier works, including the "Little Organ Book" or *Orgelbüchlein* (BWV 599-644), Passacaglia in C minor (BWV 582), and the Chromatic Fantasy and Fugue in D minor (BWV 903); also additional sacred cantatas.

1709 First pianoforte (Bartolomeo Cristofori in Florence)

1710 Birth of Giovanni Battista Pergolesi

1712 Birth of the future Prussian King Frederick II

1714 Birth of Christoph Willibald Gluck; G. W. Leibniz's *Monadology*

1715 Death of France's King Louis XIV

1717 Births of Johann Joachim Winckelmann and Johann Stamitz; François Couperin's "L'art de toucher le clavecin"

1717-1723 5 August 1717: Bach called as court capellmeister in the court of Prince Leopold of Saxe-Anhalt-Cöthen; trips in company with the prince (Dresden, Kassel, Carlsbad); compositions for the royal chamber music, including the six Brandenburg Concertos (BWV 1046-51) and the four Orchestral Suites (BWV 1066-69); works for clavier, including early versions of the two- and three-part *Inventions and Sinfonias* (BWV 772-801) and the *Well-Tempered Clavier* (BWV 846-69). 7 July 1720: Burial of Maria Barbara Bach. 3 December 1721: Bach's marriage with Anna Magdalena Wilcken. January to March 1723: The *St. John Passion* (BWV 245), with its first performance on Good Friday 1723, in the St. Thomas Church in Leipzig.

1719 Completion of the Dresden Operahouse (Pöppelmann); founding in Leipzig of Breitkopf Publishing House (after 1795, Breitkopf & Härtel)

1721 Georg Philipp Telemann called to Hamburg as music director

1722 St. Thomas cantor Johann Kuhnau dies in Leipzig; Jean-Philippe Rameau's "Traité de l'harmonie"

1723-1750 J. S. Bach as cantor of St. Thomas and director of music in Leipzig

1724 Birth of Friedrich Gottlieb Klopstock

1726 Antonio Vivaldi's *The Four Seasons*

1729 Birth of Gotthold Ephraim Lessing

1729-1735 Great choral compositions: *St. Matthew Passion* (1729, BWV 244); B-Minor Mass (1733, BWV 232); *Magnificat* (1723, BWV 243); *Christmas Oratorio* (1734-35, BWV 248); six motets (BWV 225-30).

1732 Birth of Joseph Haydn; Johann Gottfried Walther's "Musical Lexicon"

1733 First performance of Pergolesi's "La serva padrona" in Naples; Wilhelm Friedemann Bach as court organist in Dresden

1735 5 September; Birth of son Johann Christian

1736 19 November; Bach named as royal Saxony "Court Compositeur"; Sperontes (= Johann Sigismund Scholze) publishes in Leipzig his collection of *galant* songs "The Singing Muse on the Pleisse"

1737 Johann Adolph Scheibes's weekly *The Critical Musician* begins

1738 Lorenz Mizler founds the Society of the Musical Sciences in Leipzig

1739 Johann Mattheson's textbook *The Complete Capellmeister*

1740 Accession to the throne of Frederick II of Prussia; refounding of the Prussian court orchestra (C. P. E. Bach as chamber harpsichordist); Maria Theresa becomes empress; beginning of the War of the Austrian Succession (until 1748)

1741 Handel's oratorio *Messiah*

1742 Opening of the Berlin Opera House with Carl Heinrich Graun's "Caesar and Cleopatra"

1742 ff. Late contrapuntal works: Goldberg Variations (1742, BWV 988); "Canonical Variations on the Christmas Chorale 'From Heaven Above'" (1746–47, BWV 769); *Musical Offering* (1747, BWV 1079); the *Art of the Fugue* (1749-50, BWV 1080)

1744 Birth of Johann Gottfried Herder

1745 Refounding of the Mannheim court orchestra under Johann Stamitz by Elector Carl Theodor von der Pfalz. 7-8 May: Visit to King Frederick the Great of Prussia in Potsdam. In this year Bach became a member of Leipzig's Society of the Musical Sciences, founded by Lorenz Mizler

1748 Completion of the Sans Souci Palace in Potsdam

1749 Birth of Johann Wolfgang Goethe

1750 Last compositions, including the organ chorale "Before Thy Throne Herewith I Come." 28 July: Bach dies in Leipzig. 30 July: Interment in the St. John's cemetery.

Index of Illustrations

6 Interior of the St. George Church in Eisenach. Here Johann Christoph Bach (1642-1703) served as organist. In the baptismal font (foreground) Johann Sebastian was baptized on 23 March 1685.

1 Road to Wechmar. Here Veit Bach (d. 1619) lived and worked as a miller and baker. It is reported that this ancestor of the Bach family performed on a "cythringe" (a kind of lute). Before J. S. Bach's time the family had already produced twenty-seven cantors, organists, town pipers, and court musicians.

7 View of the tower and façade of the Ehrenstein palace in Ohrdruf. After the death of his father, Johann Sebastian lived in Ohrdruf 1695-1700 in the home of his older brother, Johann Christoph the younger (1671-1721). As a member of the gymnasium choir Johann Sebastian would have been in the palace for musical performances.

2 Johann Ambrosius Bach (1645-95), the father of Johann Sebastian, who was born in 1685 as the eighth child of his father's marriage with Elisabeth née Lämmerhirt (1644-94). From 1671 the father was active as court trumpeter and town piper in Eisenach. Anonymous oil painting. Eisenach, Bachhaus.

8 Interior view of St. Michael's Church in Lüneburg. Here Johann Sebastian sang in the matins choir as a scholarship student 1700-2 in the Latin school of the wealthy St. Michael's cloister. Oil painting (after 1700) by Joachim Burmester. Lüneburg, Museum.

3 The Bach House in Eisenach. The supposed birthplace of Johann Sebastian has been designated as a commemorative site.

4 Room with a four-poster bed in the Bach House in Eisenach.

9 The palace of Celle under Duke Georg Wilhelm of Braunschweig-Lüneburg was a cultural center, especially for Italian and French music, which Johann Sebastian came to know on visits from Lüneburg. Engraving by E. Willmann after a painting by G. Osterwald.

10 View of Hamburg from the east. Painting by Gabriel Engel, 1648. Hamburg, Museum für Hamburgische Geschichte.

5 Room in the Bach House in Eisenach.

11 Jan Adams Reinken (1623-1722), organist of St. Catherine's Church in Hamburg. Bach visited him from Lüneburg, and in 1720 Reinken expressed enthusiastic praise for Bach's organ playing on the occasion of Bach's audition in Hamburg. Oil painting by Gottfried Kneller (1646-1723). Hamburg, Museum für Hamburgische Geschichte.

12 View of Sangerhausen. In the summer of 1702 Johann Sebastian applied without success for the organist post here in St. Jacobi Church. In 1737, upon Bach's recommendation, his son Johann Gottfried Bernard (1715-39) was employed here as organist.

13 The Weimar Palace. From March to August 1703, Johann Sebastian was employed as a lackey and court musician in the orchestra of the coregent Duke Johann Ernst of Saxe-Weimar (1664-1707).

14 Johann Sebastian Bach. Painting (c. 1715) by the Weimar court painter Johannes Ernst Rentsch the elder. Erfurt, Städtisches Museum.

15 The Bach Church in Arnstadt. Here 1703-7 Johann Sebastian served as organist and leader of the school and church choirs.

16 Organ façade in the Arnstadt Bach Church. This organ was installed 1701-3 by the Mühlhausen organ builder Johann Friedrich Wender, and tested by Johann Sebastian in July 1703. The original façade has been retained, though the organ has been repeatedly rebuilt and enlarged, and was moved to the choir loft.

17 Original console of the Arnstadt Bach Church organ, replaced in 1864. Arnstadt, Bachgedenkstätte.

18 View of the Dornheim Church where on 17 October 1707 Johann Sebastian was married to his cousin Maria Barbara Bach (1684-1720).

19 St. Mary's Church in Lübeck. Here from November 1705 to February 1706, Johann Sebastian experienced the playing of the famous organist Dietrich Buxtehude (1637-1707) and his "evening concerts." This much-protracted stay in Lübeck led to a quarrel with the Arnstadt consistory.

20 View of Mühlhausen with St. Mary's Church, a spacious five-naved church from the fourteenth century.

21 View of the organ of St. Blasius Church, the main parish church in Mühlhausen, in which Johann Sebastian served as organist 1707-8.

22 Interior of the palace church in Weimar. From the "chapel" in the upper story with the organ Bach's cantatas were sung. The church burned in 1774. Painting (c. 1660) by Christian Richter. Weimar, Staatliche Kunstsammlungen.

23 Duke Johann Ernst of Saxe-Weimar (1664-1707). Weimar, Nationale Forschungsstätten.

24 Johann Sebastian Bach. Painting by J. Jakob Ihle, c. 1720. Eisenach, Bachhaus.

25 Prince Leopold of Anhalt-Cöthen (1694-1728) was not only Johann Sebastian's sovereign but also a "prince who loved music as well as he understood it." On 17 November 1718 he was godfather to Bach's first son born in Cöthen (Leopold August). Oil painting. Cöthen, Heimatmuseum.

26 Johann Sebastian Bach memorial in the Cöthen Palace park.

27 The Cöthen Palace hall of mirrors. Here many of Johann Sebastian's works were performed.

28 Manuscript pages from the Brandenburg Concerto No. 5. Johann Sebastian composed the six so-called Brandenburg Concertos in Cöthen as a commissioned work for Margrave Christian Ludwig of Brandenburg. Berlin, Deutsche Staatsbibliothek.

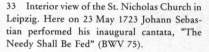

29 View of the New Augustus Palace in Weissenfels. In February 1729, Johann Sebastian received the title of "Most Royal Capellmeister of Saxe-Weissenfels," although he was never employed in Weissenfels. Various visits there, however, and many compositions (homage cantatas, hunt cantata) vouch for his close connection to the court of Duke Christian of Saxe-Weissenfels.

30 Organ façade of the St. Thomas Church in Leipzig.

31 Johann Sebastian Bach. Painting by Elias Gottlob Haussmann (1746). Bach thought highly of this portrait, the prototype for many copies and reproductions. In Bach's hand are pages of a canon (BWV 1076) that he submitted in 1747 for admission to the Society of the Musical Sciences. Leipzig, Museum für Geschichte der Stadt.

32 Exterior view of the St. Thomas Church in Leipzig, where after 1723 Johann Sebastian served as cantor.

33 Interior view of the St. Nicholas Church in Leipzig. Here on 23 May 1723 Johann Sebastian performed his inaugural cantata, "The Needy Shall Be Fed" (BWV 75).

34 Council chamber of Leipzig's old city hall. Here were held all the meetings relating to Johann Sebastian, and here on 5 May 1723 he signed his contract.

35 View of Dresden. Painting by Bernardo Belotto, called Canaletto (1721-80). Dresden, Gemäldegalerie. After 1731 Johann Sebastian frequently traveled to Dresden for organ concerts. On his recommendation his son Wilhelm Friedemann became organist of the Sophia Church in Dresden in 1733.

36 Friedrich August II (1696-1763), elector of Saxony and king of Poland (August III). He named Johann Sebastian "Court Compositeur" on 19 November 1736. Oil painting. Leipzig, Ratsstube im Alten Rathaus.

37 Page from the score of the *St. Matthew Passion* (BWV 244), first performed on Good Friday, 15 April 1729, in the St. Thomas Church, but revised by Johann Sebastian in 1736 and 1739, and completed in its final form in 1745. Berlin, Deutsche Staatsbibliothek.

38 Frederick II "the Great" of Prussia (1712-1786). Painting, Berlin, Potsdam-Sans-Souci, Staatliche Schlösser und Gärten. To this Prussian king Johann Sebastian dedicated his *Musical Offering* (BWV 1079), composed in 1747 upon a theme by the king. Bach had been in Berlin in the summer of 1741, visiting his son Carl Philipp Emanuel, who since 1740 had been employed by the king as chamber harpsichordist. During his 1747 visit he gave an organ concert in the Potsdam Garrison Church and, on 7 and 8 May, several improvisation concerts at Sans Souci.

39 Music salon in Sans Souci Palace.

40 Pages from the score of the *Art of the Fugue* (BWV 1080), on which Johann Sebastian worked in the year of his death. Berlin, Deutsche Staatsbibliothek. In the background a vault of the St. Thomas Church in Leipzig.

41 Johann Sebastian Bach. Anonymous picture in his old age, after 1748.

42 Wilhelm Friedemann Bach (1710-84). Pastel drawing. Eisenach, Bachhaus.

43 Carl Philipp Emanuel Bach (1714-88). Pastel drawing. Eisenach, Bachhaus.

44 Johann Christoph Friedrich Bach (1732-95). Painting by D. G. Matthieu, 1744. Berlin, Deutsche Staatsbibliothek.

45 Johann Christian Bach (1735-82). Painting by Thomas Gainsborough.

46 Grave marker of Johann Sebastian Bach in Leipzig's St. Thomas Church. Johann Sebastian was first buried in the St. John's cemetery, in 1900 was interred in a crypt in St. John's Church, and in 1949, after that church's destruction in the war, found his final resting place in the St. Thomas Church.